Demonic Possession Trial

Demonic Possession On Trial

✦

Case Studies in Early Modern England and Colonial America, 1593-1692

William W. Coventry

Writers Club Press
New York Lincoln Shanghai

Demonic Possession On Trial
Case Studies in Early Modern England and Colonial America, 1593-1692

All Rights Reserved © 2003 by William W. Coventry

No part of this book may be reproduced or transmitted in any form or by any means, graphic, electronic, or mechanical, including photocopying, recording, taping, or by any information storage retrieval system, without the written permission of the publisher.

Writers Club Press
an imprint of iUniverse, Inc.

For information address:
iUniverse, Inc.
2021 Pine Lake Road, Suite 100
Lincoln, NE 68512
www.iuniverse.com

ISBN: 0-595-26589-8

Printed in the United States of America

To all those who openly proceeded against the tide
of public opinion in an endeavor to
discredit the accusations
and trials of alleged witches

It may cast some Light upon the Dark things now in America, if we just give a glance upon the like things lately happening in Europe. We may see the Witchcrafts here most exactly resemble the Witchcrafts there; and we may learn what sort of Devils do trouble the World.

Reverend Cotton Mather
Wonders of the Invisible World (1693)

Contents

Introduction: Possession in History 1

Two Families in Conflict: The Possessions at Warboys 9

Possession, Puritanism, and Politics: The Cases of John Darrell &
    Mary Glover. 21

The Anne Gunter Case: An Ill Girl, a Perfidious Father, And a
    Skeptical King 35

Executions, Evidence & the Intellectual Elites: The Trial at Bury
    St. Edmunds 47

The Foreshadowing of Salem: The Goodwin Children & A
    Hanging in Boston. 59

Salem: The Self-Destruction of a New England Community by
    Possession and Panic 67

Conclusion: Common Patterns And Unanswered Questions 85

Endnotes. 99

Bibliography 129

Acknowledgements

This book is based upon the thesis I wrote in 2001-2002 to earn my Master of Arts in History from the University of Vermont. I sincerely wish to thank the people who helped me along in a variety of ways to make this book possible. I am especially grateful to my thesis advisor, Professor James Overfield, who shepherded the project from initial idea to finished thesis. I would also like to thank my other defense committee members, Professors Dona Brown and Anne Clark, for their guidance and support.

In addition, I am grateful to the Franklin and Marshall College's Interlibrary Loan staff, Mary Shelley and Jennifer Buch, for their outstanding efforts in acquiring the necessary materials for me. I would also like to thank Maureen Roat, who diligently proofread each chapter of my thesis, and particularly my brother-in-law, Brad Asher, for his insightful suggestions for both the thesis and book.

For prompt and valuable replies to my e-mail questions, I would also like to thank Victor Lucas (the present owner of the Warboys mansion), Reverend Stephen Leeke (the present pastor at the Warboys church), and historian/authors James Sharpe, Michael MacDonald, Gilbert Geis, and Ivan Bunn.

Finally, heartfelt thanks to my mother, Linda Coventry, for her words of encouragement and patience.

Introduction: Possession in History

> ...These Children were bitten and pinched by invisible agents; their arms, necks, and back turned this way and that way, and returned back again, so as it was impossible for them to do of themselves, and beyond the power of any Epileptick Fits, or natural Disease to effect. Sometimes they were taken dumb, their mouths stopped, their throats choaked, their limbs wracked and tormented so as might move an heart of stone...[1]

Describing the courtroom drama unfolding at Salem, Massachusetts in 1692, the clergyman Jonathan Hale was deeply moved by the afflictions of the young, female victims of witchcraft. Like most spectators, he found their sufferings genuine, heartrending, and undeserved. Simultaneously experiencing violent convulsions, the girls cried out in terror as specters, invisible to others, tormented them. The girls pulled pins out of their bodies, claiming witches had pushed them in. They mimicked the gestures of their tormentors, vividly demonstrating the presence of witchcraft. Their agonies were so convincing that a panic ensued, with neighbor testifying against neighbor in a torrent of accusations. Before the Salem "witchcraze" was over, nineteen people had hanged, one had been crushed to death by stones for failure to testify, and several died in prison. Salem had been torn apart.

The Salem episode is but one example of how participants might interpret and act upon cases of possession. The striking symptoms of the afflicted and the confrontational courtroom dramas, however, were nothing new. In fact, similar trials had occurred sporadically throughout the sixteenth and seventeen centuries on both sides of the Atlantic. Though historians differ in their interpretations of many aspects of these trials, they agree on one point: the afflicted girls did not determine the outcome of the trials, although they frequently played a key role. What really mattered was the response of the adults. Family and friends, and soon physicians, clergymen, and magistrates attempted to heal the afflicted, interpret the meaning behind the possession, and punish those responsible for the suffering. Adults determined whether a trial would take place, and once the trial began, adults would determine its outcome. Outcomes could vary from acquittal to conviction and hanging.

This is the focus and thesis of my paper. It examines actual possession cases, including the 1692 episode at Salem, to demonstrate this multiplicity of outcomes, each determined by unique circumstances, personalities, and issues. I have chosen these specific trials for their ability to reveal the diverse factors affecting possession cases, even though these examples shared certain stereotypical characteristics beyond the afflictions, such as the ages of the accusers and their socio-economic status compared to those they accused. The Warboys case, which the historian George Kittredge calls "…the most momentous witch-trial that had ever occurred in England," is clearly notable, as it produced the archetype for possession trials throughout the next century, as young girls' sufferings and their vivid accusations of witchcraft led to hangings.[2] The Darrell case demonstrates the manipulation of unstable young people into faking possession to dramatically promote a religion. The Mary Glover case illustrates contemporary medical theories concerning possession-like symptoms, and how divided the physicians were, depending on their political/religious orientation and allies. Brian Gunter's exploitation of his daughter's afflictions reveals how a possession case could be used for personal reasons, such as revenge. For many intriguing and idiosyncratic reasons, the events at Salem present the darkest and deadliest example. From analyzing these case studies, I can form generalizations about possession, which are presented in the conclusion.

How a society interprets and reacts to possession cases reflects its cultural characteristics, intellectual perceptions, popular beliefs, and laws. It also depends on the values and beliefs of the individuals involved. In order to explore this idea, this paper will discuss and analyze several case studies of possession that demonstrate the wide variety in how victims were treated and trials conducted. After an introductory chapter on the phenomenon of possession in history, I will analyze several examples of demonic possession in England and colonial America during the late sixteenth and seventeenth centuries. A final chapter will present my conclusions about possession and the accompanying witchcraft trials.

Demonic possession refers to the belief that a maleficent supernatural force or being can enter and dominate an individual. It has existed throughout history. The Babylonians incorporated demonic possession into the Code of Hammurabi (ca. 2000 B.C.). Ancient Greeks, Assyrians, Egyptians, and Jews all believed that spirits or demons could inhabit individuals, for good or evil. The influential Greek physicians Hippocrates (460-377 B.C.) and Galen (129-216 A.D.) rejected possession as an explanation for physical and mental disorders, which they believed resulted from a humoral imbalance.[3] Many other Greek physicians, however, continued to regard supernatural factors, such as demonic possession and prayers to Asclepias (the Greek god of medicine), as genuine.[4]

Two conditions are necessary for a possession to occur. Though it appears obvious, the first is that the culture itself must believe in the possibility of possession; it must believe that a supernatural being can inhabit a person.[5] The second precondition is that those who are supposedly possessed must adhere to a set of culturally sanctioned set of behaviors, behaviors that are essentially learned. As historian Brian Levack comments, "Demoniacs in all societies act the way their religious culture tells them they should act."[6]

Since examples of possession and the casting out of demons existed in the Bible and patristic literature, employing scriptures to understand

and treat the affliction became customary during the medieval and early modern periods. In the New Testament, both Jesus and the disciples dispossessed "unclean spirits" from afflicted individuals. These events are discussed in Mark 5. 2-13; Mark 9. 16-28; Mathew 17. 14-20; Luke 8. 27-33 and Luke 9. 37-43. Although most of these New Testament accounts emphasize the need for faith for dispossession, no specialized ceremony for exorcism existed. Jesus ordered the demons to depart and they did. Significantly, nothing in the Bible states suggests that human beings had any role in causing possessions.[7]

During the Middle Ages, a distinctive European view of demonically possessed persons and their behavior developed. Possessed individuals were usually girls or female adolescents who experienced convulsions; loss of speech, hearing, or appetite; abnormal body strength; breathing problems; hallucinations; violent disgust directed at sacred objects; and abnormal vocalizations.[8] They frequently experienced feelings of being pinched, bitten, or pricked or being insensible to pain. They sometimes appeared to understand languages they had never heard or studied, and occasionally, they vomited pins or other objects.[9] This presented the sufferer's family with a truly terrifying situation. As historian Barbara Rosen writes, "The sudden emergence, in a docile and amenable child, of a personality which raves, screams, roars with laughter, utters dreadful blasphemies and cannot bear godly utterances—or alternatively, withdraws into complete blankness—seems, even today, like the invasion of an alien being."[10]

Several of these symptoms and behaviors, however, were also characteristic of many female medieval mystics and saints.[11] Contemporaries disagreed whether God or Satan motivated an individual to display such traits.[12] Due to this uncertainty, these possessed individuals did not automatically receive veneration or respect; in fact, many were viewed with deep suspicion and repugnance.[13]

Some of the possessed truly believed a spirit or spirits had entered their body. Others, ill for apparently no reason and perhaps swayed by a physician's diagnosis of the supernatural, found demonic possession perfectly possible in the medical/theological understanding of the day. Some seemed to enjoy the theatrics and attention. Some of them were manipulated into feigning possession for profit, revenge, or power by unscrupulous parents or clergy.[14]

Important and powerful people almost never became possessed. As the psychologist and author Nicholas Spanos comments concerning the afflicted in early modern Western Europe, "Those who became demoniacs were usually individuals with little social power or status who were hemmed in by numerous social restrictions and had few sanctioned avenues for protesting their dissatisfactions or improving their lot."[15]

Contemporaries believed there were three possible explanations for causes of possession-like symptoms: fakery, illness, or actual demonic possession. How they interpreted the causes of possession naturally shaped their response to it. These categories, however, were not always precisely delineated. An illness, for example, could lead to demonic possession, as Satan could theoretically exploit the infirmity. Alternatively, a natural illness could be manipulated into a so-called supernatural affliction for fraudulent or malicious purposes, as we will see. Assorted motivations on the part of both the spectators and the possessed included political, religious, or social manipulation, greed, intense spirituality, malice, frustration, and even desire for attention.

When faced with such symptoms with no discernible natural cause or cure, people occasionally diagnosed witchcraft. They would identify, accuse, and try a witch (usually, but not always, an elderly and troublesome woman). In the belief system of the day, the witch was responsible for the affliction. To decipher these extraordinary cases, people called on doctors, clergymen, and magistrates. Authors wrote "demonologies," as new laws were promulgated to judge these unusual cases. As author and professor G.S. Rousseau wrote:

> Meticulous courtroom procedures were developed throughout Europe to winnow true demoniacs and witches from those erroneously or falsely accused—those whose prima facie manifestations of

possession were due to other causes—to illness, accident, suggestion, or even fraud. Expert witnesses were heard, especially physicians; often these were the same physicians who were compiling medical definitions of hysteria.[16]

Early modern European possession cases fall into two categories. The first involves a group of possessed individuals, often nuns. The second involves only one or perhaps a few possessed people (usually siblings). In both situations, the possessed tended to be young girls living in a strict religious environment.

Early modern France had the greatest number of group possessions. A succession of politically and religiously motivated public "show trials" exploited cases of possession between 1562 and 1642.[17] In many cases, these trials attempted to demonstrate the righteousness of Catholicism against the evils of Protestantism.[18] Nuns played a large role in many of these dramatic exorcisms and trials.[19] Trials involving possessed nuns occurred at Aix-en-Provence (1611), Lille (1613), Loudun (1634), and Louviers (1642).[20] The most famous case occurred at Loudon from 1630-34. Powerful enemies of Father Urbain Grandier accused him of bewitching the entire Ursuline convent at Loudun, including the Mother Superior. Though Grandier was well connected, his opponents conspired to stage-manage the nuns and exorcisms, forge evidence, and use political influence for revenge. He was burned alive at the stake on August 18, 1634.[21]

One noticeable difference between the French possessions at the convents and the "afflictions" occurring in England and colonial America was the lurid sexual theatrics of the French nuns. They raised their habits, begged for sexual attention, used vulgar language, and made lascivious movements. At Loudon, a local doctor, Claude Quillet, considered the disorders "…hysteromania or even erotomania. These poor little devils of nuns, seeing themselves shut up within four walls, become madly in love, fall into a melancholic delirium, worked upon by the desires of the flesh, and in truth, what they need to be perfectly cured is a remedy of the flesh."[22] English trials were much less prurient.

This thesis will concentrate on the English and colonial American trials in which only one or a few possessed individuals were involved, albeit at Salem approximately dozen girls and others were afflicted. Some were simple cases of fraud, others had grander and more complex intentions, still others were influenced by either local concerns or national issues and controversies.

After this introduction, we will look at the case of the Throckmorton children, occurring at Warboys, England from 1589 to 1593. It provides an ominous template of a repertoire of recognizable and socially understood behaviors that we will see repeatedly throughout the trials discussed in the thesis.

Chapter Three will explore the political, religious, and medical implications and tensions surrounding two possession cases that shared several of the same participants. Based in Nottingham and London between 1597 and 1602, the William Somers and Mary Glover cases involved some the most powerful members of the Anglican hierarchy in attempts to disprove their demonic possessions.

Chapter Four will bring to light another category of possession cases, that of deliberate fraud. In 1604-5, Brian Gunter beat, drugged, and threatened his daughter Anne to fake possession to avenge himself upon his neighbors. Once again, the case created a controversy. Several of the same members of the Anglican hierarchy, as well as Doctor Edward Jorden, who had been present at the Mary Glover trial, examined young Anne Gunter. Anne, a pawn in her father's plot, even found herself cross-examined by a skeptical King James I.

Chapter Five illustrates how a judge, Sir Matthew Hale, renowned for his wisdom and compassion, and a well-respected physician/essayist, Sir Thomas Browne, could contribute to the execution of two elderly widows for bewitchment at Bury St. Edmunds. The following chapter describes the events leading to the hanging of the widow

Glover in Boston for witchcraft. This episode unfortunately influenced the atmosphere and the decisions made at Salem four years later.

Chapter Seven will look at events in Salem. The chapter demonstrates how English colonists arriving in America brought with them their fundamental beliefs and traditions concerning witchcraft. First, we will look at several examples from the trials that demonstrate the diverse ways the adult community interpreted these cases. We will also examine the unique and multiple problems Salem experienced which allowed the community to be so receptive to its beliefs in Satan and witchcraft at such a late date.

By examining these cases in depth, we can get a sense of the people and relationships involved. We can also gain a sense of the dynamics of possession cases, since all these cases are in some ways unique. We have Sir Robert Throckmorton forcing Alice Samuel to live at his manor to obstruct her from afflicting his children; Judge Anderson manipulating a jury by proudly stating, in front of several members of England's medical elite, he had more than two dozen witches hanged; King James I disbelieving and helping to disprove Anne Gunter's fraudulent symptoms; Reverend John Darrell accused of tutoring disturbed teenagers to act possessed; Dr. Edward Jorden testifying Mary Glover's suffering was due to a natural illness—not possession, and later repeating the diagnosis for Anne Gunter; Judges Hawthorne and Corwin turning back the jury's decision to acquit Rebecca Nurse…these are people who shaped individual examples of possession. Their stories are both interesting and significant, for they genuinely had life or death consequences.

Two Families in Conflict: The Possessions at Warboys

From 1589 to 1593, events occurred in Warboys, England that presented a frightening and influential paradigm for seventeenth-century possession cases. The youth and gender of the afflicted, their unusual physical and mental symptoms, the doctor's diagnosis of witchcraft, the spreading of the fits to others, the credence given to children's testimony, and the executions at the end provided a model for some future trials.

Nothing quite like it had occurred before. Folk beliefs, childhood illnesses, and social antagonism coalesced to create highly dramatic confrontations with deadly consequences. The affected children exhibited an assortment of unusual behaviors that sustained an antagonism between two families for a remarkable three and a half years. As historian D.P. Walker wrote, "...this is certainly a case of considerable importance, in that it was known to later demoniacs and their healers, and is the first notorious instance of possessed children and adolescents successfully hunting witches to death."[23]

Unlike other trials, the events at Warboys were unaffected by certain larger issues. No religious rivalries impinged on the case; no political agendas or economic competitions were involved. There was no personal vendetta between the involved families before the witchcraft accusations. No medical controversy existed, as the consulting doctors agreed with each other's diagnosis. No concerted efforts were made to test the girls for "counterfeiting." The case stood solely on the symptomatology of the children and the families' reactions to them.

The parish of Warboys, Huntingdonshire, is seven and a half miles northeast of Huntingdon and eighty miles north of London. A small village at the time of the trial, its population surpassed one thousand only after 1800.

All our information about the trial comes from one widely read pamphlet published a year after the trial in 1593.[24] Entitled *The Most Strange and Admirable Discoverie of the Three Witches of Warboys, arraigned, convicted, and executed at the last Assizes at Huntington, for the bewitching of the five daughters of Robert Throckmorton Esquire, and divers other persons, with sundrie Divellish and grievous torments*, it describes the conflict between the powerful Throckmorton family and the Samuel family, accused of bewitching the Throckmorton girls. The pamphlet appears to have had several anonymous authors, nearly all members of the Throckmorton family who had participated in the events themselves. Possible co-authors included in-laws such as Gilbert and Henry Pickering (brothers of Elizabeth Throckmorton, Robert's wife) and the local minister, Reverend Francis Dorington (an Anglican minister and Robert Throckmorton's brother-in-law).[25] Naturally, their pamphlet presented only the Throckmortons' version of the events.[26]

The Throckmortons moved into their Warboys manor house on September 29, 1589. The pamphlet does not state from where or why, though we know that Gabriel Throckmorton, Robert's father, had purchased the manor in 1540.[27] Robert Throckmorton presumably lived somewhere else during his youth, possibly Ellington and Brampton, though Reverend Dorington christened the Throckmorton children at the Warboys church from 1574 to 1583.[28]

Robert Throckmorton was a close friend with Sir Henry Cromwell, one of the most prosperous commoners in England and grandfather of the renowned Oliver Cromwell.[29] Of the approximately seventy families living at Warboys, the Throckmortons were the wealthiest.[30] Members of the extended family wielded considerable influence at the

Elizabethan court.[31] In contrast, the Samuels, the family of the accused witches, were among the poorest.[32]

The conflict between the families began within six weeks of the Throckmorton's arrival. According to the anonymous author of the Witch of Warboys pamphlet:

> About the 10th of November in the year 1589 Mistress Jane, one of the daughters of the said Master Throckmorton being near the age of 10 years [she was in fact 9 years and 3 months] fell upon a sudden into a strange kind of sickness of body, the manner whereof was as followeth. Sometimes she would sneeze very loud and thick for the space of half an hour together, and presently as one in a great trance or swoon lay quietly as long; soon after she would begin to swell and heave up her belly so as none was able to bend her or keep her down; sometimes she would shake one leg and no other part of her, as if the palsey had been in it, sometimes the other; presently she would shake one of her arms, and then the other, soon after her head, as if she had been infected with the running palsey.[33]

The parents first believed this to be a natural illness, possibly epilepsy, which they called the "falling sickness."[34] Witchcraft was mentioned for the first time when their elderly neighbor, Alice Samuel, called on the sick girl at the manor, and Jane accused her of being a witch. Jane's mother, embarrassed, rebuked Jane, and sent her to her room, but a tenuous association between Jane's illness and Mrs. Samuel had been established.

Seeking a medical explanation for their child's afflictions, the Throckmortons called upon two respected Cambridge physicians, Drs. Barrow and Butler (whose first names are not given in the pamphlet). As was then common, the physicians only examined Jane's urine, not Jane herself. After four such examinations, with no improvement from Jane, both physicians diagnosed witchcraft.[35] There was one problem however: since the Throckmortons were new to the area, they claimed to have no enemies who would have had a reason to bewitch their daughter.

Within a month, the four other Throckmorton daughters fell ill with similar symptoms of sneezing and violent convulsions. According to the pamphlet, they were "…being deprived of all use of their senses during their fits, for they could neither see, hear, nor feel anybody, only crying out of Mother Samuel, desiring to have her taken away from them, who never more came after she perceived herself to be suspected."[36] After the doctors' diagnosis, the children's symptoms sufficiently alarmed the parents to make them consider witchcraft as a cause. Their suspicions were strengthened after the girls experienced fits when Reverend Dorington prayed for them.

On February 13, 1590, Gilbert Pickering forced Alice Samuel, her daughter Agnes, and Cicely Burden (about whom nothing is known except she was a suspected witch) to the Throckmorton manor to undergo a "scratch" test by Jane Throckmorton while several members of the Throckmorton family observed. According to folk beliefs, scratching a witch reputedly alleviated the bewitched person's afflictions. Such a result would also confirm the witch's guilt. Jane refused to scratch either Cicely or Agnes, believing them not responsible for her suffering. However, Jane scratched Alice, "…with such vehemency that her nails brake into spills with the force and ernest desire that she had to revenge."[37] Both Jane and Alice Samuel tumbled to the floor as Jane's violent scratching failed to bring relief. Master Whittle, a friend of the Throckmortons, attempted to restrain the girl:

> …but not long after they were thus fallen to the ground, the said Master Whittle took up one of the said children, which was Jane Throckmorton, and carried her into an inward chamber, laying her upon a bed; and being a man of as great strength as most be this day in England, and the child not above nine years old, yet he could not hold her down to the bed, but that she would heave up her belly far bigger and in higher measure for her proportion than any woman with child ready to be delivered, her belly being as hard

as though there had been for the present time a great loaf in the same; and in such manner it would rise and fall an hundred times in the space of an hour, her eyes being closed as though she had been blind and her arms spread abroad so stiff and strong that the strength of a man was not able to bring them to her body.[38]

Fearing their proximity to Alice Samuel was harming the girls, the day following the scratch test, February 14, Robert Throckmorton sent his children away from Warboys to live with relatives. Elizabeth Throckmorton, aged about fourteen, resided at the home of Gilbert Pickering. Here, Elizabeth stated she saw the spectral image of Alice, "…in a white sheet with a black child sitting on her shoulders which makes her tremble all over, and she calls on uncle Master Pickering and others to save her…"[39] Elizabeth also claimed the specter tried to force a demon, variously described as either a cat, mouse, or toad, into her mouth.[40] Elizabeth also began to react violently when she heard scripture readings. According to the pamphlet, "…any good word (if any chanced to name God, or prayed God to bless her, or named any word that tended to godliness)," caused fits to occur.[41]

After the children failed to improve from living a month at their relatives' homes, they returned to Warboys. Shortly thereafter, in March 1590, Lady Cromwell, the wife of the Samuels' landlord and a friend of the Throckmortons, and her niece visited the Throckmortons. Almost immediately, the children exhibited their symptoms. Lady Cromwell sent for Alice Samuel and, upon arrival, berated Samuel for causing the girls' affliction. An argument ensued in which Lady Cromwell grabbed a pair of scissors, cut off a lock of Alice's hair, and gave it to Mrs. Throckmorton to burn. Like scratching, this was a folk remedy to weaken a witch's power.[42]

Insulted by Lady Cromwell's attack, Mrs. Samuel asked, "Madam, why do you use me thus? I never did you any harm as yet."[43] That very night, Lady Cromwell dreamt a terrifying nightmare about Alice Samuel. She consequently fell ill and died slightly more than a year later, in July 1592. The Throckmorton children accused Alice Samuel of having caused Lady Cromwell's death, suspicions confirmed by Alice's ominous "...as yet," spoken after the original altercation. The "murder" of Lady Cromwell eventually legitimized the executions of the Samuels, as the Witchcraft Act of 1563 allowed capital punishment of convicted witches if their actions resulted in death.[44]

Between Lady Cromwell's visit and her death, another confrontation occurred which heightened suspicion of Alice Samuel. Around Christmas, 1590, Henry Pickering, a scholar, and two other Cambridge students met her near a pond. They accused Alice Samuel of bewitching the Throckmorton children. Samuel angrily denied the accusations and declared that if she had "wanton" children acting in this manner punishment would certainly follow. Pickering replied if she had harmed the children, "...he hoped one day to see her burned at a stake, and he himself would bring fire and wood and the children would blow the coals."[45] Alice finished the confrontation with "I had rather see you doused over head and ears in this pond."[46]

Combined with her threat against Lady Cromwell, this heated exchange held a deeper significance than just angry words. In the sixteenth century, people greatly feared curses and threats from an alleged witch.[47] Not only did the person cursed often believe the threat might work, but the witch could have as well.[48] In fact, the subsequent death of Lady Cromwell appeared to substantiate Samuel's reputation as a witch.

For the next two years, the children continued to experience afflictions and accuse Alice Samuel. As the adult Throckmortons implored her to confess, Alice refused. Then in autumn, 1592, the children's symptoms worsened.[49] They saw gowns and rings floating in air, and fell into violent fits at the tolling of church bells. By now, the Throckmortons were convinced that witchcraft was causing their daughters' troubles.

The girls began to speak in strange voices, supposedly those of demons once commanded by Alice Samuel to harm them. Then in the fall of 1592, these demons decided to work against Mrs. Samuel.

According to *The Most Strange and Admirable Discoverie of the Three Witches of Warboys*, "Towards All Hallowstide [Oct. 31] the spirits grew very familiar with the children, and would talk with them half an hour together...about the manner of fits they should have, and concerning Mother Samuel...the spirits said many times that they would bring her to shame in the end."[50]

The children decided upon what appears to be a strange course of action. They convinced their parents that their health would improve if Alice Samuel resided at the Throckmorton manor. They explained that this odd arrangement would make it impossible for Alice to feed or communicate with her imps, thus weakening her power. The children told Alice Samuel "that they shall not be well in any place except in her house, or she be brought to continue with them; and besides that, they shall have more troublesome fits than ever they had..."[51] For the next three weeks, into December, 1592, the children "...had very many most grievous and troublesome fits; insomuch that when night came, there was never a one of them able to go to their beds alone, their legs were so full of pain and sores, besides many other griefs they had in their bodies..."[52]

Robert Throckmorton hesitantly realized Alice would have to live in his household. He offered Alice's husband, John, ten pounds to hire the best servant in Huntingdonshire in return for letting her reside at the Throckmorton manor.[53] Samuel refused, and for one day, Robert had the children live at the Samuel's small residence. John Samuel threatened to freeze and starve the children, but finally relented to his powerful neighbor's coercion to let his wife live at the Throckmorton's. For the next ten days or so, while Alice Samuel found herself living in this strained situation, the children showed no signs of illness.[54]

This unusual state of affairs demonstrated the children's power over their father as they manipulated him into this extraordinary and uncomfortable decision, which in turn upset the living arrangements for the entire Samuel family. In no other possession case was the suspected witch coerced into living in the home of the afflicted.

Though the girls exhibited several frightening physical ailments (convulsions, great strength, etc.), they also demonstrated what could be considered childish willfulness and behavior. Refusals to listen to prayers and readings from the Bible, and stubbornness over eating habits, are actions today that may be considered childhood rebellion. One of the sisters, Elizabeth ate only if taken to a nearby picturesque pond.[55] According to the pamphlet, Elizabeth, "...delighteth in play; she will pick out some one body to play with her at cards, and but one only, not hearing, seeing or speaking to any other..."[56]

Soon, even the new living arrangements proved unsatisfactory for the children. They accused Alice of feeding the spectral imps (which only they could see) when no one was looking, and once more they began to experience fits, even in Alice's presence. The imagination, whims, and sufferings of the children now fully controlled their parents and in-laws.

The presence of specters foreshadowed the spectral evidence so important at the Salem witch trials almost exactly a century later. Unlike the terror the Salem specters produced, however, Joan Throckmorton easily conversed with her spirits. Named Blue, Pluck, Catch, and three Smacks (who were cousins), and supposedly sent by Mrs. Samuel, they were said to control Joan's fits. Doctor Dorington, the rector of Warboys and Robert Throckmorton's brother in law, noticed this dialogue.[57] Apparently talking to herself, since no one else could see the spirits, she would says things such as, "...What doest thou say...that I shall now have my fits when I shall both hear, see and know everybody? That is a new trick indeed!"[58]

For almost the remainder of 1592, Alice Samuel lived at the Throckmorton's in an uncomfortable situation. Robert Throckmorton came to believe Alice could predict when the fits would occur. With the children present, and though she was "very loath" to foretell anything, Robert pressured her into revealing when his daughters would experience fits.[59] The children behaved just as she had predicted. Not surprisingly, this prophecy made Alice appear even guiltier.

Finally, the emotional stress became too much for Alice. Well aware of the effect her presence had upon the children's health and behavior, Alice might have come to believe that she was responsible. She broke down and confessed on December 24, 1592 at the Throckmorton's home and again at church the following day. Upon hearing this, her horrified husband and daughter forced her to retract her confession. Not only had she shamed the Samuel's family name, but she could now be prosecuted.

Alice's retraction angered and embarrassed Throckmorton, whose stature and reputation could not countenance such a reversal. He told Alice, "I will not let pass this matter thus; for seeing it published, wither you or I will bear the shame of it in the end."[60] With neighbors secretly posted by Throckmorton near an open window, Reverend Dorington wrote down yet another confession by Alice. When John Samuel arrived to discover that his wife had confessed again, this time in writing and in front of witnesses, he called her "…a foul term—and would have stricken her, had not the others stood betwixt them."[61] Alice again desperately tried to recant her confession.

The Samuels' bickering over Alice's confession resulted in all three becoming suspects, which corresponded to the common belief that witchcraft ran in families. On March 25, 1593, at the Throckmorton manor, Joan Throckmorton, Jane's older sister, scratched Agnes Samuel's cheeks until bloody. With the Throckmorton children present, Agnes also stumbled over reciting the Lord's Prayer and Creed, something Robert Throckmorton had ordered her to do.[62] Though this was enough to prove the Samuels' guilt to Robert Throckmorton, he realized that to erase all doubts of the Samuel's guilt he would have to take them to court. This period of adult recriminations, confessions, and retractions, with dramatic fits and outbursts from the children, lasted until April 1593.

On April 4, 1593, the trial took place at nearby Huntingdon, with Judge Edward Fenner presiding. According to the pamphlet, at least five hundred people viewed the proceedings.[63] The children continued their fits until each member of Samuel family stated, with slight variation, "As I am a witch and did consent to the death of the Lady Cromwell, so I charge the devil to suffer Mistress Jane to come out of her fit at this present."[64] Though Alice and Agnes stated the oath promptly, John Samuel refused to acknowledge his guilt until Judge Fenner threatened him with immediate execution unless he confessed to witchcraft. Upon hearing the Samuels' oaths, the children immediately became well. With the oaths and the children's reaction, Judge Fenner ordered the Samuels hanged.

The significance of the Warboys case lies in the peculiar behavior of the girls, the influence of the trial and the pamphlet, and its deadly outcome. The fame of the Warboys witches inspired other cases, most notably the case of Anne Gunter in 1608. The historian George Kittredge calls the Warboys case "...the most momentous witch-trial that had ever occurred in England," partially because it "...demonstrably produced a deep and lasting impression on the class that made laws."[65] He makes a strong case that the Warboys trial influenced the passage of the Witchcraft Bill of 1604.[66]

For the purpose of our paper, we find in this witchcraft trial a classic example of how personalities can shape and interpret a possession. Free from outside influences such as religious and political controversies, the Throckmortons and their in-laws, apprehensive over the children's health, employed a series of tests to ascertain the guilt of those responsible for harming the girls. For *years*, folk remedies such as scratching and burning articles of the witch's clothing were employed. The Pickering brothers tried threats and tests against Alice Samuel to alleviate the children's suffering. Dr. Dorington attempted to heal the children through prayer. Paradoxically, some of these tests, such as scratching Alice Samuel or burning her hair, proved she was not a witch, as the children steadfastly continued to exhibit symptoms.

Only after nearly four years of confrontations and afflictions did the case go to trial. Armed with Alice Samuel's confession and his family's testimony, Robert Throckmorton won the court case. As predicted by the folk belief of the day, the death of the witches healed the bewitched. The children recovered once they heard the verdict, and the Samuels hanged on April 6, 1593.

Possession, Puritanism, and Politics:
The Cases of John Darrell &
Mary Glover

Although the Warboys trial involved highly placed members of English society, and may have contributed to the Witchcraft Act of 1604, the next case study we will consider surpassed it in notoriety and influence. Widely known and discussed throughout London, the Mary Glover/Elizabeth Jackson trial occurred in 1602. Prominent members of the English religious and political elite, as well as several members of the Royal College of Physicians, played roles in this case. The question whether Elizabeth Jackson bewitched Mary Glover into suffering convulsions, dumbness, blindness, throat constrictions, and other afflictions became a matter of great interest. According to the historian Michael McDonald, the trial "...captured the attention of London's leading citizens, enraged the church hierarchy and alarmed the government."[67]

Two issues connected with the trial were especially controversial. The first issue concerned the religio-political implications of a possession case during the late Elizabethan/early Jacobean period. The second centered on medical issues of the case. As in most possession cases, physicians were consulted to diagnose Mary Glover's affliction, and in this instance, their diagnoses became the subject of divisive debates.

Because the significance of the Mary Glover/Elizabeth Jackson trial is rooted in the larger religio-political controversies affecting England at the time, some background information is necessary. Although a detailed analysis of the issues and effects of the Reformation and Counter-Reformation is beyond the scope of this paper, it is important to underscore that England did not escape the tensions and conflicts associated with sixteenth-century Europe's struggles for religious supremacy. In fact, conflicts between Catholics and Protestants and between contending Protestant groups created major internal and external problems for Queen Elizabeth I (r. 1558-1603).

Pope Pius V excommunicated Queen Elizabeth in 1570, promising absolution to anyone who assassinated her. In response to the pope's decree, fines and laws against Catholics in England became harsher. Elizabeth's Catholic cousin, Mary, Queen of Scots, conspired to overthrow Elizabeth by means of a Catholic insurrection in England and with the help of Philip II, the Catholic King of Spain. Elizabeth reluctantly had Mary beheaded in 1587, and in 1588 Elizabeth's navy destroyed Philip's Spanish Armada. Elizabeth remained securely on the throne with Anglicanism as the national religion, and conformity to the doctrines and practices of the Church of England became a type of litmus test for loyalty to the Queen.

By the late 1580s, conflicts also arose between the Anglicans, led by Queen Elizabeth I and the Archbishop of Canterbury, John Whitgift (1583-1604), and the Puritans, over issues such as predestination, the wearing of liturgical vestments, and the similarity of many Anglican ceremonies to those of the Catholic Church. The Puritan movement, which wanted the Anglican Church to distance itself from Catholicism, began in the mid-1550s, when a group of Marian exiles (English Protestants who fled England due to persecution by Queen Mary) visited John Calvin in Geneva. Upon their return to England around 1560, they attempted to further "purify" the Church by adopting strict Calvinistic doctrine, especially in regards to predestination.[68]

One of the dramatic issues dividing the Anglicans, Catholics, and Puritans, particularly critical to the Glover case, was the concept of demonic possession. All three groups shared the belief that evil spirits could possess individuals, but they disagreed about the best method to cast out such demons. Using different techniques, justified by different beliefs and supporting biblical verses, Catholics and Puritans employed exorcisms and public dispossessions, respectively, to heal the afflicted and attract converts.[69] Exorcism is a Catholic rite that employs sacred words, holy names, prayer, confession of faith, and the use of holy water to expel demons.[70] The Puritans employed prayer and fasting for their dispossessions. People of the time, however, used the terms rather indiscriminately. Any means of casting out a spirit can be called a dispossession. All exorcisms are attempts at dispossession, but not all dispossessions use this specific Catholic ritual.

By the 1580s, cases involving demonic dispossession were becoming symbolic weapons for use on theological battlegrounds. After Catholicism and Catholic exorcisms were declared illegal and driven underground, Anglican doctrine became more skeptical of demonic possession.[71] This ran against certain Puritan beliefs, however, which regarded dispossession as a way to aid the afflicted and authenticate their doctrines.[72]

While the Anglican hierarchy of the late sixteenth century encouraged prayer and fasting to seek God's guidance or request his help in times of need, Puritans transformed this idea into highly publicized sessions of prayer and fasting for possession cases. These might involve the participation of several ministers and last for several days. Smaller sessions usually occurred around the bedside of the afflicted, while larger ones took place outdoors in great public displays of religious enthusiasm. The climax of Catholic exorcisms and Puritan dispossessions was usually a dramatic confrontation between the possessing spirit and the exorcist/minister. This tended to establish and elevate the power and reputation of the individual minister or priest. During the turbulent and occasionally dangerous battle for the hearts and souls of England, specifically 1570-1603, whichever faith manifestly cured the afflicted appeared to be the "true Church." Possession cases served a striking and effective proselytizing function.

The Anglican hierarchy rejected the Catholic rite of exorcism as superstitious, ineffectual, and "popish," and Puritan dispossession ceremonies as fraudulent and theatrical. They viewed exorcisms and dispossessions as futile attempts to compel a supernatural being to act a certain way if priests or ministers performed specific procedures, an impossible degree of power for humankind.[73] The Anglican hierarchy believed that miracles such as dispossession occurred during the time of Jesus and the Apostles to prove the divinity of their mission, but were no longer necessary for an established church of the late sixteenth and seventeenth centuries.[74] This disagreement over religious doctrine helps explain the controversy over the dispossession of a young girl from a Puritan family named Mary Glover.

Before we discuss the Glover case, we must first examine the judicial environment in which it occurred. Several of the people involved in her case were also involved in the activities of the well-known Puritan dispossessor, John Darrell.[75] Darrell first became a problem to the Anglican religious authorities in 1596, when he dispossessed thirteen-year-old Thomas Darling, the "Boy of Burton," who had been afflicted with convulsions, sacrilegious speech, rolling eyes, moaning, and cries of torment. After a doctor diagnosed bewitchment by examining Darling's urine without examining Darling himself, Darling described a woman he believed had bewitched him, whom his family recognized as Alice Goodridge, a woman from a nearby town whose mother had a reputation for witchcraft. Friends and family of Darling examined Alice as a possible witch. Goodridge was unable to repeat the words of the Lord's Prayer, a characteristic of witches, and admitted to missing communion for over a year. Both seemed to confirm her guilt.[76]

This led to a trial presided over by Sir Edmund Anderson, whose severe anti-Puritanism had been well known since judging an earlier case against a radical Puritan group called the Brownists in 1581.[77] Anderson also firmly believed in witchcraft and the possibility of demonic possession. After Goodridge's conviction, Anderson sentenced her to a year in prison, the maximum penalty for a first offence of witchcraft under the 1563 Witchcraft Act. As she languished in jail, where she would die before completing her sentence, Darrell managed to cure Darling by prayer and fasting.

Darrell's dispossession of Darling, along with a pamphlet describing the event entitled *The Most Wonderfull and True Storie of a Certain Witch named Alse Gooderige* (London: 1597),[78] brought Darrell to the attention of the Anglican hierarchy. In the wake of this case, powerful Anglicans, including the Archbishop of Canterbury, John Whitgift, the bishop of London, Richard Bancroft, and his chaplain Samuel Harsnett, tried to enforce doctrinal conformity by discrediting Darrell. They had his pamphlet destroyed and the printer, along with several of Darrell's supporters, imprisoned.[79] These Anglican opponents of Darrell later were involved in the Glover trial as well.

The following year, in 1597, Darrell dispossessed seven young members of the household of Nicholas Starkey in Cleworth, Lancashire. A "cunning man," Edward Hartley, originally hired to cure the afflicted children, was accused of breathing demons into the children by kissing them, and subsequently was hanged as a witch. Darrell and his co-worker, Reverend George More, arrived after the hanging and dispossessed the children.[80]

In early November 1597, as a sign of his growing reputation, Darrell was called to Nottingham by concerned townspeople to dispossess twenty-year-old William Somers, who in 1591 suffered fits with symptoms suggesting epilepsy.[81] Six years later, Somers again experienced these afflictions and fell into spectacular and occasionally obscene fits (one included bestiality with a dog), in front of reportedly one hundred and fifty witnesses. At this time, unnamed worshippers had given Darrell and Somers written accounts of the Warboys trial.[82] The ideas behind some of Somers afflictions and accusations may have come from these sources.

Somers blamed several local women for bewitching him, which led Darrell to boast that Somers could expose all the witches in England. His apparently successful dispossession of Somers led spectators to invite Darrell to be a preacher at St. Mary's Church, Nottingham.[83] After Darrell accepted the offer, to his discomfiture, Somers's possession returned. By late November, Darrell's relentless preaching against devils, along with blaming the sins of the towns for the boy's repossession, created fear and factionalism in Nottingham that lasted for approximately five months.[84]

Distressed by this crisis, Darrell's critics in Nottingham notified Archbishop Whitgift of Canterbury of Darrell's disruptive activities. Whitgift discussed the dispute with Bancroft, who had Somers interrogated by the mayor and three alderman of Nottingham, in January 1598.[85] Somers at first confessed that Darrell had tutored him and others into feigning possession. Darrell, in turn, successfully persuaded Somers to recant his confession, but on March 31, 1598, Somers again confessed to fraud.[86]

The Archbishop of Canterbury summoned Darrell and More to Lambeth Palace, his residence, where they were imprisoned while awaiting trial for counterfeiting possessions. Chief Justices Sir John Popham and Sir Edmund Anderson, both strong opponents of Puritanism, presided, with Samuel Harsnett as the chief prosecutor.[87] Thomas Darling and William Somers testified that Darrell had tutored them to simulate possession. In May 1599, the court deposed Darrell and More from the ministry and imprisoned them. It appears, however, they were out of jail within a year or two.[88]

Though the court documents no longer survive, we can ascertain a reasonably accurate picture of what occurred from the more than thirteen pamphlets and books, published between late 1598 and 1601, that discussed the Darrell trial, many in direct response to each other.[89] Immediately after the trial Harsnett wrote a full-length book entitled *Discovery of the Fraudulent Practises of John Darrell* (1599), which criticized Darrell's ability to dispossess. As a professed Christian, Harsnett could not attack the belief in Satan or possession itself. Instead, he concentrated on demonstrating the theatricality and fraudulence of dispossessions and exorcisms. In 1600, Darrell responded with his *A*

Detection of that Sinnful and Ridiculous Discours of S. Harshnet, a line-by-line repudiation of Harsnett's book.[90] After a year or two in which minor pamphlets of questionable authorship from the Darrell side appeared, Darrell himself published no more, despite the ongoing debate.

All these events and controversies provide the background for the Mary Glover case. In the spring of 1602, Bancroft and Harsnett heard of the alleged bewitchment of a fourteen-year old Puritan girl named Mary Glover. The case came at a critical time for England, and this explains why it drew the attention of so many influential people. With Queen Elizabeth dying, people wondered how James VI of Scotland, presumably the next king of England, would treat Puritans.[91] The interpretation and possible manipulation of Glover's possession could validate competing religious positions during an uncertain time.

The quarrels and opinions over the Glover possession have survived in three pamphlets, all published within a year of the trial. Two of these, Dr. Bradwell's *Mary Glovers Late Woeful Case* and John Swan's *A True and Brief Report of Mary Glovers Vexation*, argued that Mary Glover had been bewitched.[92] The third pamphlet, *A Brief Discourse of a Disease called Suffocation of the Mother*, by Dr. Edward Jorden, argued there was a rational, medical explanation for her symptoms. He testified at the trial that Mary suffered from the "suffocation of the mother," a disease similar to hysteria. Though Jorden did not discuss the trial in *A Brief Discourse*, he did elaborate on the symptomatology of "suffocation of the mother."[93]

According to one of the authors, Stephen Bradwell, a member of the College of Physicians, the possession began in April 1602, when fourteen-year-old Mary Glover, a London shopkeeper's daughter, gossiped about her neighbor, the elderly widow, Elizabeth Jackson.[94] According to Bradwell, on hearing of Mary's gossip, Jackson confronted Mary Glover at Jackson's house, and "…rayled at her, with many threats and cursings, wishing an evill death to light upon her."[95] Bradwell does not say why Mary was at the Jackson home, but does state that Mary was terrified by the confrontation and told a neighbor she was feeling unwell before returning home.

For the next eighteen days, Mary experienced dumbness, blindness, throat constriction, abdominal distortions, sudden unconsciousness, and convulsions. Mary's parents at first believed their daughter was ill. Unlike Jackson (about whom virtually nothing is known, other than being a "charewoman"), the Puritan Glovers had powerful connections, in that Mary's uncle, William Glover, was an alderman and former sheriff.[96] They asked Thomas Moundeford, who later served as President of the College of Physicians seven times, to examine Mary. Dr. Moundeford concluded at first she was suffering from an unidentified, but natural, disease.[97] Jackson, however, reportedly boasted to several people, including Alderman Glover, that she had caused Mary's illness, saying, "I thank my God he hath heard my prayer, and stopped the mouth and tyed the tongue of one of myne enemies."[98]

This state of affairs naturally distressed Mary's mother, who confronted Jackson. Jackson angrily denied the allegations that she was a witch and threatened Mary's mother with, "You have not crosses ynow, but I hope you shall have as many crosses, as ever fell upon woman and Children."[99] Jackson's threats and curses only intensified the Glovers' antagonism and suspicions.

This inspired family and friends of the Glovers to coerce Elizabeth Jackson into a series of staged experiments with Mary over the next several months. Jackson enlisted the aid of her neighbors to prove her innocence while supporters of the Glovers hoped these confrontations would either heal Mary or prove Jackson's witchcraft.[100] To see if Mary was sensitive to pain (insensitivity confirmed a supernatural affliction), experiments took place to illicit a physical response, which included applying hot pins to Mary's cheeks and burning paper to her hands. Mary displayed no signs of pain. In another experiment, Elizabeth slipped into Mary's presence while in disguise. Mary responded by falling into fits. When in Jackson's presence, Mary threateningly intoned "hang her, hang her" in a nasally voice.

This encouraged more people to come to see the experiments, which occurred at several homes, including those of her uncle. Professor Michael Macdonald describes one such event as follows, "The house was jammed with people: pious Puritans awestruck by the evident power of Satan, more skeptical observers wanting to see for themselves whether Glover's illness was natural or supernatural and the merely curious."[101] These spectators argued amongst themselves about the true cause of the afflictions. With these experiments attracting increasing numbers of observers, city authorities began to be concerned about these strange events. London's chief legal officer, Recorder John Croke, repeated the experiments at his lodgings at the Inner Temple.[102] Once Croke decided Mary's afflictions resulted from witchcraft, Jackson was indicted.[103] According to Professor MacDonald, Croke promoted the dispossession of Glover that followed her trial and was possibly a Puritan himself.[104]

The trial, which occurred on December 1, 1602, revealed a conflict in the presiding judge, Edmund Anderson. A staunch anti-Puritan, as demonstrated in the Darrell trial, he was also a staunch opponent of witchcraft. Would the verdict exonerate the possessed Puritan or the accused witch? Though he worked with Bancroft on earlier trials, Anderson did not share the powerful bishop's skepticism towards possession.[105] Nor was there any way to gauge the jury's inclination. More tests occurred at the trial to determine whether Mary was "dissembling." A repeat of the burning test helped authenticate her possession:

> After dinner the Lo. Anderson Mr. Recorder of London, Sir William Cornwallis, Sir Jerome Bowes, and diver other Justices went up into the Chamber, to see the mayde; before whome went the Towneclerke, with som officers; with thundring voyces crying; bring the fyre, and hot Irons, for this Counterfett; Come wee will marke her, on the Cheeke, for a Counterfett: but the senseles mayde apprehended none of these things. After the Justices had considered the figure, and stiffenes of her body, Mr. Recorder againe [Fol. 32r] with a fyred paper burnt her hand, until it blistered. Then was Elizabeth Jackson called for, At the instant of

whose coming into the Chamber, that sound in the maides nostrils, which before that time, was not so well to be distinguished, seemed both to them in that Chamber, and also in the next adjoining, as plainely to be discerned, *Hang her*, as any voice, that is not uttered by the tongue it selfe can be…The Lord Anderson then commanded Elizabeth Jackson to come to the bed, and lay her hand upon the maide; which no sooner was done, but the maides body…was presently throwen, and casted with great violence. The Judge willed the woman to say the *Lordes prayer*; which by no means she could go through with, though often tryed…"[106]

The court turned to Elizabeth Jackson next. Asked to recite the Lord's Prayer, Jackson stumbled over the words. Jackson's misspoken lines drove Mary into convulsions. For the spectators, this observable linkage between Jackson's mistakes and Mary's convulsions demonstrated Jackson's guilt.

Following Jackson's examination, Jorden and Dr. John Argent, later to be President of the College of Physicians eight times, testified that Mary suffered from a natural disease, "the suffocation of the mother."[107] According to contemporary medical belief, the womb (the "mother" in the terminology of the day) caused these symptoms by wandering throughout the body, disturbing other organs such as the brain, heart, and liver.[108] Observed for centuries, the symptoms of "suffocation of the mother" included choking (with frightful throat swellings), convulsions, weeping, paralysis, and unnatural vocalizations.

Jorden, however, refused to say he could cure Mary Glover. In a humiliating rebuke to Jorden's diagnosis of Glover's symptoms, according to which Jackson could not possibly be responsible for bewitchment, Judge Anderson stated: "Divines, Phisitions, I know they are learned and wise, but to say this is naturall, and tell me neither the cause, nor the Cure of it, I care not for your Judgement: geve me a naturall reason, and a naturall remedy, or a rash for your physic."[109]

Though Judge Anderson despised Puritans, he was particularly proud of his record against witches. In his jury summation, he stated,

"This Land is full of Witches…I have hanged five or six and twenty of them…This woman [Jackson]…is full of cursing, she threatens and prophesies and still it takes effect; She must of necessitie, be a Prophet or a Witch."[110] The jury agreed with the judge. Jackson received the maximum sentence for a first time conviction of witchcraft, one year in jail and four stands at the pillory.[111] There is no record, however, of her having served the sentence.[112]

Two weeks later, on December 14, 1602, Mary Glover was finally cured during an all-day session of fasting and prayer in which several Puritan ministers battled the devil.[113] Whether Mary's afflictions were encouraged and co-opted by the Puritan acquaintances of the family, or whether the Glovers were the catalyst behind the dramatic trial and dispossession, is simply unknown.

At the dramatic conclusion, Mary's performance enthralled the spectators as she cried out with the same words her grandfather (burned during Marian persecutions) had declared at the time of his death.[114] As the Puritan pamphleteer John Swan[115] wrote:

> …the maid did fall down suddenly into the chair, where she remained without motion, her head hanging downward, somewhat inclining toward the shoulder, her face and color deadly, her mouth and eyes shut, her body stiff & senseless, so as there were that thought, and I think we all might have said, *behold she is dead*…After she had continued a while in this deadly state: suddenly in a moment, life came into her whole body, her mouth and eyes opened, and then lifting up her hands and stretching them wide asunder as high as she could reach, the first word she uttered was, he is come, he is come (looking backward (with a very comfortable countenance) on some of the preachers, and then on such as stood on each side of her) *the comforter is come, O Lord thou hast delivered me*.
>
> As soon as her father (who stood not very nigh) heard her so cry: he also cried out and said (as well as his weeping would give him leave) *this was the cry of her grandfather going to be burned.*[116]

Though Mary and her supporters won a momentary propaganda victory by proving the effectiveness of Puritan dispossessions, they soon lost the larger conflict. The publicity surrounding the trial, the pamphlet war, and the controversy inflamed by this test of religious effectiveness against Satan led to the downfall of Puritan dispossessions.

Immediately after the trial, Jorden, Swan, and Bradwell published their three pamphlets. Jorden's *A Brief Discourse of a Disease Called the Suffocation of the Mother* developed the analysis of the disease he had presented during his trial testimony. According to Professor Michael MacDonald, Bishop Bancroft almost undoubtedly commissioned the pamphlet to promote the bishop's religious viewpoints.[117] From the Puritan viewpoint, Bradstreet and Swan's pamphlets describing the trial had to be published secretly, without the name of a publisher, to avoid Bancroft's censorship.[118]

This case is significant in two ways, one that was apparent then, and one that became evident later. It demonstrated how religious rivalries, medical uncertainties, and political complexities affected a witchcraft trial. Though the powerful Anglican hierarchy attempting to sway the jury with their use of highly respected physicians, it could not dictate the verdict. Judge Anderson firmly pushed the jury's verdict against Jackson, but he certainly was not a Glover supporter. While the Puritan allies of Mary Glover hoped public dispossessions would result in converts to their faith, the Anglicans under Bancroft decided to crush this type of proselytizing by outlawing these troublesome public dispossessions. In 1604, in the *Constitutiones sive Canones Ecclesiastici*, enacted by the Anglican Convocation, Canon 64 stated a minister's bishop would have to give permission to clergymen to perform any dispossession.[119] Penalties for performing a dispossession without permission included suspension for the first offense, excommunication for the second offence, and removal from the ministry for the third offense. Bishops avoided the possession controversy by apparently never giving permission to clergymen for dispossessions.[120]

The second significant point is that Edward Jorden's attempt to undermine the theory of supernatural causation for illness mirrored the Anglican hierarchy's attempt to reject the existence of miracles and demonic possession.[121] Such opinions slowly took hold and would eventually lead to skeptical beliefs concerning witchcraft. Yet, few people at the time accepted their rationalistic, "modern" viewpoints. Not only did possessions, witchcraft accusations, and executions for bewitchment continue, but as colonists English Puritans took their beliefs across the Atlantic.

This case demonstrates that attitudes towards demonic possession did not easily fade away. At the very beginning of the sixteenth-century, a convicted witch in London suffered a minor punishment for bewitchment. At the end of the century, in Salem, Massachusetts, nineteen people hanged for the same offense, proving that even though strong attempts to eradicate concepts such as demonic possession occurred throughout the seventeenth century, the belief in the supernatural remained credible, as well as dangerous.

The Anne Gunter Case:
An Ill Girl, a Perfidious Father,
And a Skeptical King

Witchcraft legislation in England changed significantly between the trial of Mary Glover in 1602 and that of Anne Gunter in 1604-6. King James I (1566-1625), who ascended the throne in 1603 after having served as king of Scotland, traditionally has been considered the catalyst for these new laws.[122] James, however, was not personally involved in drafting Parliament's Witchcraft Act of 1604, though he participated in several witchcraft cases that were subject to this legislation.[123]

As king of Scotland, James VI was initially zealous in his prosecution of witches. In 1590, he came to believe a coven of witches raised ferocious storms in an attempt to assassinate him and his new bride while the royal couple sailed between Denmark and Scotland. Since the threat was against James and his queen, the accused stood trial for treason as well as witchcraft and sorcery.[124]

During these trials, held at North Berwick, James originally believed the witches were either lying or deluded about their powers. He changed his mind when one of them recounted the confidential conversation he had with his wife on their wedding night. Depositions stated three hundred witches supposedly met and concluded a pact with the Devil.[125] The prosecution accused them of making and melting wax figures of James and riding the sea in sieves. James personally interrogated the accused and supervised the torture of the witches. He also heatedly overrode a jury's acquittal of Barbara Napier, one of the witches accused at the trial.[126] James had several of the accused burned at the stake.

In 1597, James published his influential treatise, *Daemonologie*, a compendium of existing beliefs on witchcraft that asserts that witches could raise storms and cause illness. In the book, James advocated the "swimming" test for witchcraft, which, like torturing suspected witches, was illegal in England.[127] He also expressed the contemporary belief that women were more predisposed to evil than men were.

After his accession to the English throne, however, James gradually became more skeptical of witchcraft accusations.[128] He personally exposed a number of frauds, notably that of the thirteen-year-old John Smith, the "Leicester Boy," in 1616. Unfortunately, by the time James personally exposed the hoax, the magistrates had already hanged nine of the accused.[129] Witchcraft accusations in England declined during this period, perhaps due to James' influence.[130] During his twenty-two year reign in England, less than forty executions for witchcraft took place.[131]

Once James became king of England, English ecclesiastical and secular bodies passed new laws, which had been in the works for several years, to combat witchcraft and called for more severe sentences.[132] The Anglican Convocation enacted the Canons of 1604, which required a clergyman to receive a bishop's permission to perform any dispossession.[133] This effectively stopped the large public displays of demonic possession and dispossession that had angered the Anglican hierarchy during the previous quarter century.

More importantly, Parliament passed the Witchcraft Act of 1604, which allowed for execution of witches even if no death was involved. This was more severe than the earlier Elizabethan code of 1563, by which Elizabeth Jackson received a one-year sentence for causing Mary Glover's illness by bewitchment. Entering into a diabolical pact with the devil also became a punishable offense under the 1604 law.

One of the first trials tried under this new law concerned the bewitchment of an approximately twenty-year-old young woman named Anne Gunter. Unlike the Darrell and Glover cases, personal religious enthusiasm did not play a part in her possession. The Anne

Gunter case serves to illustrate another possibility for the motivation behind possession cases, namely fraud, in this case, perpetrated by Anne's father, Brian Gunter, a relatively wealthy gentleman, who directed and publicized the possession.

The Gunters lived in North Moreton, Berkshire, a small village of only a few hundred people twelve miles south of Oxford.[134] The richest man in North Moreton, Brian Gunter, had a reputation for litigiousness.[135] He had been feuding continuously with the Gregory family since 1598, when during a melee after a football match, he mortally wounded two Gregory cousins. Although Gunter avoided a formal charge of manslaughter (no doubt due to his status), the Gunter and the Gregory families became adversaries.[136]

As observed in previous trials, fraud was always a possibility in possession cases. Friends and family of the afflicted at first rarely believed the sufferers were demonically possessed and instead sought a natural explanation. In many cases, a physician, unable to cure the patient, suggested demonic possession caused the symptoms. Tests of the afflicted by the clergy and magistrates followed the physician's diagnosis. Previous "counterfeit" possessions were exposed and publicized, making fraud a reasonable assumption in any trial. Anne Gunter, however, did a remarkable job of sustaining the deception from late October 1604 until late February 1606, when she finally was "found out" by King James and his advisors.

The trouble began in mid-summer 1604, when Anne fell ill with what appeared to her father as either "suffocation of the mother," hysteria or "falling sickness," epilepsy.[137] Only months before, from August 1603-February 1604, North Moreton had lost over fifty people due to the bubonic plague, so any sickness must have been particularly frightening.[138] After this brief illness, she recovered until late October 1604, when a relapse occurred and the symptoms worsened.

Brian took his daughter to several physicians, none of whom helped her. Her symptoms came to include temporary blindness and deafness, long fasts, convulsions, trances, voiding pins from her orifices (including nostrils), and foaming at the mouth. Anne's strange ailment interested others in the county, interest Brian actively encouraged. The vicar of North Moreton, Gilbert Bradshaw, stated that in her fits Anne could "...declare and tell matters & speeches done & spoken privately & further did disclose & describe divers persons with their several habits and apparel which were to come unto her before they came or were seen of any."[139] According to the Gunters' neighbor, Nicholas Kirfoote, Brian Gunter "sent for most of the parish of Moreton to see and behold his daughter Anne in her fits."[140]

By December 1604, the Gunters and the spectators gradually began to see witchcraft as the cause for Anne's afflictions. Anne envisaged the specters and the spectral familiars of three women, Agnes Pepwell, her illegitimate daughter Mary, and Elizabeth Gregory.[141] Anne knew these women well. All had reputations in the community as witches, especially Agnes Pepwell.[142]

The community of North Moreton apparently considered Elizabeth Gregory bad-tempered and contentious. As Reverend Bradshaw stated, she was "...accounted a scold & an unquiet body amongst her neighbours & a great curser & swearer..."[143] Her husband, Walter, like Brian Gunter, also had a reputation for litigiousness. Walter Gregory and Brian Gunter, however, were never adversaries in court, though they had lived in the same small town for over seventeen years.[144]

Members of the clergy attempted to resolve the conflict. Though we do not know the exact date, at some point in late 1604, Reverend Bradshaw brought Anne and Elizabeth Gregory together. Gregory's angry condemnations of both Anne and Reverend Bradshaw only exacerbated the situation.[145] In addition, in late 1604, three other clergymen, Reverends Chetwyn, Whetcombe, and West, came to pray and fast with Anne, but their bishop Henry Cotton, following the strict Anglican guidelines recently passed in the Canons of 1604, refused to give his permission for a dispossession.[146] They provided some comfort but failed to cure her.

As Anne's afflictions continued, Alice Kirfoote, wife of Nicholas, began to believe she was bewitched as well. Reverend Edward Sampson from Kingston said Alice experienced "...a great rising or swelling in her belly, her neck & mouth also drawn awry, her eyes fixed in her head...& her joints like iron & she could not be made to bend or move any way."[147] We do not know the specific date for Alice's illness, but it was probably December or January. Alice also blamed Elizabeth Gregory, whom she disliked intensely,[148] and Agnes Pepwell for her illness. Later, however, Anne Gunter testified that Alice Kirfoote worked with Brian Gunter to promote Anne's fraudulent possession, so Kirfoote's illness certainly appears suspicious.[149]

During the winter of 1604-5, Brian Gunter acted with his neighbors against the unpopular and suspect women. They attempted folk remedies such as burning the thatch of the Gregory and Pepwell homes, and locks of the women's hair, which temporarily alleviated Anne's symptoms. Anne moved around to live in a variety of homes, which provided some relief.[150]

Neighbors also compelled meetings between the accusers and the accused, in hopes of curing the afflicted women's symptoms and defusing the neighborhood acrimony. In one of these encounters between Anne and Elizabeth, an enraged Elizabeth railed that Brian Gunter "...was a murdering bloodsucker & that the blood of the Gregorys should be revenged upon the blood of the Gunters, & she would have blood for blood."[151] Not surprisingly, these meetings only exacerbated the fits and further convinced the neighbors that the accusations were true.

Brian Gunter also enlisted the aid of his son-in-law, Thomas Holland, the regius professor of divinity at Oxford and rector of Exeter College, early in Anne's illness, probably in November 1604.[152] Several Oxford dons, who met with Anne at the request of Holland, agreed with Gunter's accusations against the women. Oxford physicians and medical students who allied themselves with Gunter included Bartholomew Warner, Roger Bracegirdle (a fellow of Brasenose College),

Robert Vilvaine (MA), and John Hall (MA).[153] Other Oxonians who witnessed Anne's afflictions included John Prideaux (future regius professor of divinity, rector of Exeter College, vice chancellor of Oxford three times, chaplain to Prince Henry and James I), Thomas Winniffe (future bishop and chaplain to Prince Henry and Charles I), and Dr. John Harding (regius professor of Hebrew, future chaplain to James I). Several lower level Oxford clergy also observed Anne.[154]

With several of his neighbors and members of Oxford's elite willing to testify against the accused witches, Brian Gunter requested the constable of North Moreton, Richard Spooner, arrest Elizabeth Gregory and Mary Pepwell as witches in either November or December 1604 (the record is unclear). The accused witches awaited the Abingdon assizes in nearby Reading Gaol.

Things did not go completely smoothly for Brian Gunter. At the last moment, the Kirfootes refused to press charges, leaving Brian Gunter alone. A larger, and unexpected, problem for the Gunters was the skepticism of their kinsman (the specific relation is not described),[155] Thomas Hinton. After Hinton had witnessed Anne's fits in early February 1605, Gunter had hoped Hinton would support him in the legal action against the witches. Instead, although Hinton originally agreed to help, he soon expressed skepticism over Anne's apparent fits. He knew Gunter had allied himself with powerful Oxford supporters for the trial, but felt Gunter should avoid, "…the guilt of innocent blood" by continuing with the trial.[156]

Just days before the trial, in late February 1605, Hinton confided his doubts about Anne's possession to Alexander Chocke, the Berkshire justice of the peace. As a result, Chocke, who would also be foreman of the jury during the upcoming trial, along with two other justices of the peace, Edward Clarke and Sir Richard Lovelace, visited Anne at the King's Head Inn at Abingdon.[157] After questioning her, with several unnamed Oxonian supporters of Anne present, the justices concluded that her possession was unauthentic.[158]

With the trial of Gregory and Pepwell set for March 1, 1605, the three justices apprised the two presiding judges, Sir Christopher Yelverton and Sir David Williams, of their assessments of Anne's bewitchment. The opinions of Yelverton and Williams concerning witchcraft held a great deal of weight, as they had helped craft Parliament's Witchcraft Act of 1604.[159]

The trial took place on March 1, 1605. Brian Gunter's supporters from the community testified concerning Anne's afflictions and the accused witches' wicked reputations. They described their eyewitness accounts of Anne's trances, contortions, and prolonged fasting. The Oxford scholars who testified deposed that from medical and theological viewpoints Anne's afflictions were genuine and supernaturally produced. They had heard Anne cry out against the three women during her fits. They witnessed that Mary Pepwell's presence triggered Anne to fall into fits.[160] They recalled her ability to make herself heavier, her head bigger, and her body a foot taller.[161] This "evidence" proved to them the bewitchment of Anne, which in turn meant the accused women were guilty of a capital crime. Dr. John Harding, however, testified that Anne could not read in the dark, though she claimed she could read while blind.[162]

Brian and Anne Gunter also testified. Brian catalogued Anne's afflictions while Anne, supposedly in a trance, demonstrated each one in turn. Brian Gunter also asked the judges to force Elizabeth Gregory to repeat the oath the Throckmorton children had used at the Warboys trial to convict the Samuel family. Though we do not know the exact wording of the spell, it was roughly, "As I am a witch, so I charge the devil to let Miss Anne Gunter out of her fit at this present."[163] At Warboys, the Samuels stated the oath, essentially admitting their guilt, which in turn cured the children's afflictions. Elizabeth Gregory, however, did not phrase the oath perfectly, and Anne continued to writhe on the ground and curse her. This did little to convince the judges who, according to historian James Sharpe, could not have been too pleased with Brian Gunter's efforts to advise them on the proper way to run the trial.[164] The judges refused Brian Gunter's request to have Gregory read the spell again, forcing him to exclaim, according to Chocke, "…he had not that justice Mr Throckmorton had."[165]

The eight-hour trial ended in acquittal for the accused. Gregory and Pepwell returned to North Moreton, where they still lived with the stigma of witchcraft. Three days after the trial, March 4, 1605, three members of the College of Physicians examined Anne and concluded that she faked her symptoms.[166] One of these physicians was Dr. John Argent, the same man who testified at the Elizabeth Jackson trial three years previously that Mary Glover suffered from a natural disease.[167]

A few weeks after the medical diagnosis, Ann was placed under the care of Dr. Richard Haddock in Salisbury, who also concluded Anne was faking the symptoms. From then on, she would continually be under someone's care other than her father's, none of whom found the possession authentic.[168]

In late August 1605, King James I, his wife Anne of Denmark, and their son Henry visited Oxford. Employing his Oxford connections, Brian Gunter took this opportunity to appeal to James directly to retry his case. Gunter hoped the renowned witch-hunter would be more sympathetic towards his plight than the judges at Abingdon. James decided to hear the case, indicative of his personal interest in witchcraft. Unfortunately for the Gunters, James and his Anglican hierarchy by now were deeply skeptical of demonic possession.[169]

On August 27, 1605, the first day of his visit to Oxford, James allowed Brian and Anne Gunter to plead their case. Shortly thereafter, Anne was placed under the supervision of the Archbishop of Canterbury, Richard Bancroft, for evaluation. By placing Anne in his custody, James probably assumed Bancroft would uncover the fraud. According to James' friend and fellow Scot, Robert Johnson, "The archbishop, when he accomplished nothing by threats, warnings, and promises, called on the services of Samuel Harsnett, his chaplain, whom he honoured above others."[170] Harsnett, the Anglican propagandist, had been involved with Bancroft during the Darrell trial and the Mary Glover case.

While Anne was under Harsnett's care, Dr. Jorden examined her. Three years earlier, Jorden, like Dr. John Argent, had testified at the Mary Glover trial that the root of Mary's suffering was, in his opinion, "the mother," not bewitchment. Agreeing with Argent, Jorden concluded that Anne had faked her symptoms.[171]

Harsnett, reputedly acting on James' advice, arranged for a servant of Bancroft's named Asheley (about whom nothing else is known) to woo Anne. This appears to have helped Anne, in that her afflictions ceased about this time (mid-September).[172]

King James also met three more times with Anne, once at an unknown date, the others on October 9 and 10, 1605.[173] These meetings with James, the romance with Asheley, the skepticism displayed by Bancroft and Jorden, the separation from her father, along with losing the court case at Abingdon, overwhelmed her resistance to confessing to faking her possession. For her confession, James promised indemnity from prosecution and money towards marriage. James described Anne in a letter to Robert Cecil, his chief minister:

> And we find by her confession that she finds herself perfectly cured from her former weakness by a potion given to her by a physician, and a tablet hanged about her neck; that she was never possessed with any devil nor bewitched; that the practice of the pins grew at first from a pin that she put in her mouth, affirmed by her father to be cast therein by the devil...and lastly that she hath been very far in love with one Asheley, a servant to the Lord of Canterbury, and is still, hath sought his love long most importunately and immodestly (in unfit to be written) and she doth now humbly and earnestly crave our furtherance that she may marry him; and this last is confessed also by himself.[174]

During these examinations before the king, Anne described the deception. She said her father forced her to drink a mixture of sack and sallet oil, which drugged her into feeling unwell. In Samuel Harsnett's

Declaration of Egregious Popish Impostures (1603), he had described drinking a mixture of sack and sallet oil as technique Catholic exorcists employed to make a suggestible person feel possessed.[175] Anne also stated her father forced to swear an oath in church that she would never confess their secret. As for the pins, Anne stated Alice Kirfoote taught her the sleight of hand necessary to perform the deception.[176]

Though James soon found himself preoccupied with the consequences of the Gunpowder Plot (discovered November 5, 1605), proceedings against Brian Gunter for fraud began on February 24, 1606 at the Star Chamber office at Gray's Inn.[177] Court cases at the Star Chamber, however, could take years to resolve.[178] Unfortunately, the privy councilors' decree of Gunter's trial, which did not conclude until 1608, is unknown.[179]

We do know that Brian Gunter admitted to using the Warboys text, an unnamed book by John Darrell, as well as at least one of Harsnett's works (unnamed but probably *Declaration of Egregious Popish Impostures*) to gain the knowledge about possession to teach Anne how to feign her symptoms.[180] Although sentences by the Star Chamber included mutilation, imprisonment, and/or a heavy fine, it appears Brian Gunter suffered only the imprisonment awaiting trial (approximately one to two years). It is possible that like his daughter, Brian confessed to perpetrating the hoax.[181] Though we know several facts concerning Brian after his trial, Anne, however, disappears completely from any documented facts. We do not even know if she eventually married or when she died.

This case demonstrates both the credulity shown by certain members of the elite, even Oxford dons, towards demonic possession and bewitchment, as well as the skepticism shown by the Anglican religious establishment and King James himself. It illustrates how different people, local gentry, concerned neighbors, and Oxford theologians and physicians all came to different conclusions about this possession case. It demonstrates how a person might ruthlessly exploit beliefs about witchcraft for revenge, with nearly homicidal results.

Fortunately, the Anne Gunter trial proved how the new Witchcraft Act was not subverted or manipulated by a relatively powerful gentleman against his vulnerable and unpopular neighbors. In fact, the Gunter trial was a landmark case, being the first time the English government ever prosecuted the accusers of witches.[182]

Executions, Evidence & the Intellectual Elites: The Trial at Bury St. Edmunds

After examining the numerous ways people interpreted or manipulated possession cases in the previous three chapters, it is important to view the state of affairs a half century later. After the political and religious machinations of the John Darrell and Mary Glover trials, the sordid fraud of the Anne Gunter case, and the increasing skepticism of King James I, it would be understandable to believe possession trials would soon die out. Unfortunately, possession cases and witchcraft trials continued to occur sporadically throughout the century.

A three-day trial occurred at Bury St. Edmunds from March 10-13, 1662, which provides us with an interesting possession case quite free from the political coercion, religious rivalries, and the nefarious schemes of other trials we have examined. All we know about the trial is from a sixty-page pamphlet entitled *A Tryal of Witches, at the Assizes held at Bury St. Edmonds for the County of Suffolk; on the Tenth day of March 1664* (though it actually occurred in 1662). Published in London in 1682, supposedly by an anonymous spectator, this pamphlet is the sole primary source for the trial.[183]

Though the trial occurred at Bury St. Edmunds, the events leading up to it occurred in Lowestoft, an isolated fishing town with a population of about fifteen hundred one hundred and twelve miles northeast of London and fifty miles east of Bury St. Edmunds.[184] At the time of the trial, Lowestoft was involved with a lawsuit against the larger fishing town of Great Yarmouth over fishing rights, which involved two principal members of the witchcraft trial, Samuel Pacy and Sir Matthew Hale.[185]

Like many witchcraft trials, the incident that initiated the trial at Bury St. Edmunds transpired when a reasonably prosperous member of the community denied a request from a poorer one. In this instance, Samuel Pacy, a wealthy fish merchant and property owner of Lowestoft, rejected several requests from Amy Denny, a widow with a reputation as a witch, to sell her some fish. According to Samuel Pacy, whose deposition is recorded in the 1682 pamphlet, immediately after he turned down Amy Denny a third time, his daughter, Deborah "…was taken with most violent fits, feeling most extream pain in her Stomach, like the pricking of Pins, and Shreeking out in a most dreadful manner like unto a Whelp, and not like unto a sensible Creature."[186]

After Deborah's symptoms continued for three weeks, Pacy asked a neighbor, Dr. Feavor, for his opinion, but Feavor could not diagnose a natural cause of the illness.[187] Though Pacy consulted a doctor, it appears he did not seek the help of the clergy, which presents a unique absence in demonic possession trials. Nor in Pacy's deposition at the trial is there any mention of employing any religious methods of dispossession.

Samuel Pacy's deposition stated that Deborah Pacy, "…in her fits would cry out of *Amy Duny* as the cause of her Malady, and that she did affright her with Apparitions of her Person."[188] After Samuel Pacy made a formal complaint, the authorities put Amy Denny in the stocks on October 28. This, however, did not end his daughter's symptoms. According to the pamphlet, two days later "…being the Thirtieth of *October*, the eldest Daughter *Elizabeth*, fell into extream fits, insomuch, that they could not open her Mouth to give her breath, to preserve her Life without the help of a Tap which they were enforced to use…"[189]

For the next two months, the two sisters suffered other symptoms, including lameness and soreness, loss of their sense of speech, sight, and hearing, sometimes for days. Fits ensued upon hearing the words "Lord," "Jesus" and "Christ." They also claimed that Rose Cullender, another reputed witch, and Amy Denny, "...would appear before them, holding their Fists at them, threatning, *That if they related either what they saw or heard, that they would Torment them Ten times more than ever they did before.*"[190] The sisters also coughed up pins, "...and one time a Two-penny Nail with a very broad head, which Pins (amounting to Forty or more) together with the Two-penny Nail were produced in Court, with the affirmation of the said Deponent, that he was present when the said Nail was Vomited up, and also most of the Pins."[191] Allotriophagy, the vomiting of extraordinary objects, provided an observable proof of possession.[192]

As the Throckmorton family at nearby Warboys had done seventy years earlier, the parents relocated the sisters to the homes of relatives seven weeks after the initial illness in hope of a cure on November 30, 1661. While the girls lived at Margaret Arnold's house, their aunt who believed they might be faking their symptoms, she subjected them to an experiment. She removed all the pins from the children's clothes, yet, "...notwithstanding all this care and circumspection of hers, the Children afterwards raised at several times at least Thirty Pins in her presence, and had most fierce and violent Fitts upon them."[193] Margaret Arnold soon became convinced that something supernatural was causing the girls' afflictions, as well as believed the girls' allegations that bees and flies forced pins and nails into their mouths.[194]

While the children continued their fits and hallucinations at their aunt's house, an ominous event occurred when an unnamed, "...daughter being recovered out of her Fitts, declared, *That* Amy Duny *had been with her and that she tempted her to Drown her self, and to cut her Throat, or otherwise to Destroy her self.*"[195] These visions could be seen as signs of severe stress and possible mental illness, as the child affirmed her belief that spectral images were directing her to commit suicide.

The trial itself occurred on March 10, 1662. By then, the afflictions had spread to three other girls, neighbors of the Pacys: Ann Durrant (probably between the ages of 16-21), Jane Bocking (14 years old), and Susan Chandler (18 years old).[196] Deborah Pacy and Jane Bocking were too ill to attend the trial. Though Elizabeth, Ann, and Susan did not testify (family members spoke for them), they were present and affected the courtroom atmosphere. The three arrived...

> ...in reasonable good condition: But that Morning they came into the Hall to give Instructions for the drawing of their Bills of Indictments, the Three Persons fell into strange and violent fits, screeking out in a most sad manner, so that they could not in any wise give any Instructions in the Court who were the Cause of their Distemper. And although they did after some certain space recover out of their fits, yet they were every one of them struck Dumb, so that none of them could speak neither at that time, nor during the Assizes until the Conviction of the supposed Witches.[197]

The trial opened with the deposition of Dorothy Durrant. Her statement chronicled old and unprovable events. Durrant did not explain why she had waited several years to accuse Denny. She alleged Amy Denny of bewitching and eventually murdering her ten-year-old daughter, Elizabeth, four years earlier. She also testified that although her infant son, William, suffered similar afflictions, Dr. Jacobs, a physician from Yarmouth, rescued him by recommending the use of counter-magic. Dr. Jacobs told Dorothy to hang William's blanket over the fireplace and to burn anything found in it. When she took it down at night, a large toad fell out, which a boy in the house quickly caught. As he held it over the fire with tongs, the toad exploded with a flash of light.[198]

Durrant also testified that the next day, a relative of Amy Denny told her that Denny had recently suffered serious burns all over her body. According to Durrant's deposition, when she visited Denny, the burned woman cursed her and predicted that Durrant would outlive some of her children and be forced to live on crutches.

Her predictions soon proved accurate. Durrant's daughter, Elizabeth, soon fell seriously ill, and after seeing Amy Denny's specter, died. After Elizabeth's death, Dorothy Durrant became crippled in both her legs. Judge Hale, attempting to find a natural explanation for the affliction, asked her if the lameness was due to "...the Custom of Women."[199] Durrant rejected this possibility. Forced to use a crutches for over three years, she threw these away, supposedly cured, when she heard Denny and Cullender pronounced guilty.[200]

The most dramatic evidence at the trial was the presence and actions of the children. Elizabeth Pacy created quite a scene, as she:

> ...could not speak one Word all the time, and for the most part she remained as one wholly senseless as one in a deep Sleep, and could move no part of her body, and all the Motion of Life that appeared in her was, that as she lay upon Cushions in the Court upon her back, her stomack and belly by the drawing of her breath, would arise to a great height: and after the said Elizabeth had lain a long time on the Table in the Court, she came a little to her self and sate up, but could neither see nor speak..., by the direction of the Judg, Amy Duny was privately brought to Elizabeth Pacy, and she touched her hand; whereupon the Child without so much as seeing her, for her Eyes were closed all the while, suddenly leaped up, and catched Amy Duny by the hand, and afterwards by the face; and with her nails scratched her till blood came, and would by no means leave her till she was taken from her, and afterwards the Child would still be pressing towards her, and making signs of anger conceived against her.[201]

After these dramatic events, parents of afflicted children outside the Pacy home testified. They were Edmund Durrant, father of Ann, apparently no relation to Dorothy; Diane Bocking, mother of Jane; and Robert and Mary Chandler, parents of Susan. They swore that their children suffered afflictions similar as to those of the Pacy children, specifically, fit, seeing spectral images, and vomiting crooked pins.[202] They brought to the court several pins as evidence. In a deposition strikingly similar to that of Samuel Pacy, Edmund Durrant, about who nothing is known other than his deposition,[203] described the afflictions of his daughter, Ann:

> ...That he also lived in the said, Town of Leystoff, and that the said Rose Cullender, about the latter end of November last, came into this Deponents House to buy some Herrings of his Wife, but being denied by her, the said Rose returned in a discontented manner; and upon the first of December after, his Daughter Ann Durent was very sorely Afflicted in her Stomach, and felt great pain, like the pricking of Pins, and then fell into swooning fitts, and after the Recovery from her Fitts, she declared, That she had seen the Apparition of the said Rose, who threatned to Torment her. In this manner she continued from the first of December, until this present time of Tryal; having likewise vomited up divers Pins (produced here in Court). This Maid was present in Court, but could not speak to declare her knowledge, but fell into most violent fits when she was brought before Rose Cullender.[204]

Dr. Thomas Browne, a respected physician who lived relatively close by, testified next. He affirmed that witchcraft existed, specifically mentioning similar events that had occurred in Denmark. Despite mentioning possible medical explanations for the girls' afflictions, namely "the mother," Browne noted that the Devil could intensify symptoms. Though he believed that the girls were bewitched, he did not specifically state that Denny and Cullender had afflicted them. Browne testified:

> ...That the Devil in such cases did work upon the bodies of men and women, upon a natural foundation, [that is] to stir up and excite such humors, super-abounding in their Bodies to a great excess, whereby he did in an extraordinary manner afflict them with such distempers as their bodies were most subject to, as particularly appeared in these children; for he conceived, that these swooning fits were natural, and nothing else but that they call the Mother, but only heightened to a great excess by the subtlety of the

devil, cooperating with the malice of these which we term witches, at whose instance he doth these villanies.[205]

After Browne's testimony, the court carried out several experiments to test the accused witches and their accusers. In contrast to the Mary Glover case, no burning occurred to test the hands for insensibility. Here, the fists of the girls, while afflicted, remained tightly closed, "...as yet the strongest Man in the Court could not force them open; yet by the least touch of one of the supposed Witches, *Rose Cullender* by Name, they would suddenly shriek out opening their hands, which accident would not happen by the touch of any other person."[206]

Three respected members of the aristocracy, Lord Charles Cornwallis, a member of Parliament in attendance as a county magistrate, Sir Edmund Bacon, a justice of the peace for the county, and Sir John Keeling (who became Chief Justice of the King's Bench three years after the trial, to be succeeded by Hale in May 1671),[207] one of the three "serjeants," a post secondary to the judge, tested Elizabeth next. While they supervised, a blindfolded Elizabeth Pacy touched Amy Denny and another woman. When Elizabeth reacted similarly to both women, "...the Gentlemen returned, openly protesting, that they did believe the whole transaction of this business was a meer Imposture."[208] Samuel Pacy replied "...That possibly the Maid might be deceived by a suspicion that the Witch touched her when she did not."[209]

Though Pacy's explanation for the test result helped convince the jury of Denny's guilt, other factors also played a role. As the author of *A Tryal of Witches* acknowledged, many people believed that these girls were not capable of "counterfeiting":

> It is not possible that any should counterfeit such Distempers, being accompanied with such various Circumstances, much less Children; and for so long time, and yet undiscovered by their Parents and Relations: For no man can suppose that they should all Conspire together, (being out of several families, and as they

Affirm, no way related one to the other, and scarce of familiar acquaintance) to do an Act of this nature whereby no benefit or advantage could redound to any of the Parties, but a guilty Conscience for Perjuring themselves in taking the Lives of two poor simple Women away, and there appears no Malice in the Case. For the Prisoners did scarce so much as Object it.[210]

Depositions by John Soan, Robert Sherringham and Nicholas Pacy (Samuel's father or brother), followed. Significantly, all had civil suits against a John Denny during the 1640's and 1650's. By the time of the trial, Ann Denny's husband, John, was deceased. As there were two John Dennys in Lowestoft at this time, with dozens of civil cases against one or both men, it is impossible to prove that this was the same John Denny.[211]

John Soan accused Rose Cullender of bewitching his three carts, making them unusable for a day. Robert Sherringham blamed her for the loss of four horses and several cows and pigs, as well as his lameness and his suffering a "...great Number of Lice of extraordinary bigness."[212] Following their testimony, the wife of Amy Denny's landlord, Ann Sandeswell, deposed that Denny complained that her chimney might collapse, which it did a short time later. Additional testimony by Ann concerning the loss of geese and fish ended the depositions.[213]

After these witnesses spoke, Hale had the opportunity to verbally review the evidence for the jury, which he had done in past trials. He did not recapitulate in this case, "...least by so doing he should wrong the Evidence on the one side or on the other."[214] Instead, according to the writer of *A Tryal of Witches*, Hale instructed the jury:

> ...That they had Two things to enquire after. *First*, Whether or no these Children were Bewitched? *Secondly*, Whether the Prisoners at the Bar were Guilty of it?
>
> That there were such Creatures as *Witches* he made no doubt at all; for *First* the scriptures had affirmed so much. *Secondly*, The wisdom of all Nations had provided Laws against such Persons, which is an Argument of their confidence of such a Crime...*For to con-*

demn the innocent and to let the guilty go were both an abomination to the Lord.[215]

The jury took half an hour to convict both women. The spectacle of a tormented eleven-year-old girl fiercely scratching a stereotypical witch, coupled with a great deal of circumstantial evidence, appears to have convinced the jury. The men of the jury, none of whose identity is known, condemned the women to their deaths.

The following morning, the previously possessed children and their parents visited Hale. The children appeared cured, "And Mr. Pacy did Affirm, that within less than half an hour after the Witches were Convictd, they were all of them Restored, and slept well that Night, feeling no pain; only Susan Chandler felt a pain like pricking of Pins in her Stomach."[216] Denny and Cullender "were urged to confess, but would not."[217] The two hanged on March 17, 1662.

What generates special interest and significance in the 1662 trial at Bury St. Edmunds is the personal integrity, intellectual acumen, and professional achievements of some of the main participants. Renowned and respected even to this day, Sir Matthew Hale, Chief Baron of the Exchequer, presided over the trial, and Dr. Thomas Browne, knighted 1671, a celebrated author and physician, testified. Both were known for their incorruptibility and tolerance, qualities that undoubtedly helped them to not only survive, but also to prosper during these turbulent times in English history.

Sir Thomas Browne, a resident of nearby Nottingham, was at the height of his career in 1662. The author of a half dozen major works, his eclectic interests ranged from his candid personal views on religion as a physician (*Religio Medici*, 1643), to natural history (*Pseudodoxia Epidemica*, 1646) to ancient funeral rites (*Hydriotaphia*, 1658). At times skeptical, anti-dogmatic, mystical, erudite, witty, moderate, and curious, Browne and his works had many admirers. Though he dabbled with some scientific experimentation (both he and Hale wrote about magnetism, for instance), Browne, like Hale, also firmly believed in Satan and witchcraft.[218] He believed evil was a part of God's universe, and to doubt the existence of witchcraft opened the door to atheism. Two decades before the trial, in probably his greatest work, *Religio Medici* (1643), Browne had written:

> It is a riddle to me, how this story of oracles hath not wormed out of the world that doubtful conceit of spirits and witches; how so many learned heads should so far forget their metaphysics, and destroy the ladder and scale of creatures, as to question the existence of spirits. For my part, I have ever believed, and do now know, that there are witches: they that doubt of these, do not only deny them, but spirits; and are obliquely, and upon consequence a sort not of infidels, but atheists.[219]

Sir Matthew Hale, four years Browne's junior, also wrote prodigiously. Unlike Browne, Hale chiefly wrote for his own edification and enjoyment. Although he published only a few works, his posthumous *History of the Common Law of England* (1713) and *Histroia placitorum coronae* (1726) were highly regarded for centuries.[220] Principally interested in religion and the law, Hale, like Browne, commented on natural history and the relationship between Christianity and reason. Both men typified the culture of the Oxford-educated,[221] successful, well read, and well-respected Englishman at the top of his chosen profession.

Dr. Browne of Norwich appears in only one paragraph of *A Tryal of Witches, at the Assizes held at Bury St. Edmonds*. Unfortunately, neither Browne nor Hale was alive at the time of publication to review and possibly refute the pamphlet. Since neither man mentioned the experience at Bury St. Edmunds in any of their voluminous works or personal correspondence, it is impossible to discern their views towards the events.[222]

Sir Matthew Hale and Sir Thomas Browne are examples of highly intelligent people, at the apex of their respected professions, who sincerely believed in witchcraft. Hale probably presided over at least one other witchcraft case that ended with an execution.[223] In England, however, the era in which it was possible to prosecute and execute witches was ending. Educated justices found executing poor, elderly, and "outcast" women based on the testimony of children problematical. As the belief in witches slowly died out, the ability to prosecute them died out even more quickly.[224]

The real grievance against these men is that they are judged by later legal, medical, and scientific standards, not those of their own era. Edmund Gosse, a biographer of Browne, characterized his participation in the trial, "…the most culpable and the most stupid action of this life…Among the most appalling stories of witch-trials, none was more shocking, none more inexcusable than that which resulted in the hanging of Amy Duny and Rose Cullender."[225] Hale's biographer, Edmund Heward, found the omitting the summary of evidence at the end of the trial a "sign of weakness" and alleged that Hale's behavior "…indicates the credulity and superstition which mingled with his religious beliefs."[226]

Another consequence of this trial was its influence upon the events at Salem. Several features of this trial bear a remarkable resemblance to the Salem trials three decades later.[227] The crisis originated with the afflictions of Deborah and Elizabeth Pacy, whose ages, nine and eleven, were identical to those of two girls, Betty Parris and Abigail Williams, who played a key role in the Salem witchcraft trials. The symptoms of the girls and reports of witches' specters were similar in Bury St. Edmunds and Salem. In both cases, the afflictions spread to other girls, and adults contributed testimony about previous confrontations with the accused. Finally, the conclusion was the same—hangings.

In 1693, when Reverend Cotton Mather published his *Wonders of the Invisible World*, he enclosed a chapter entitled "A Modern Instance of Witches: Discovered and Condemned in a Trial Before That Celebrated Judge, Sir Mathew Hale." Mather begins, "It may cast some Light upon the Dark things now in *America*, if we just give a glance upon the *like things* happening in *Europe*. We may see the *Witchcrafts* here most exactly resemble the *Witchcrafts* there."[228] After stating that the trial was "…much considered by the Judges of *New England*,"[229] Mather summarized *A Tryal of Witches* in the next nine pages of his book.

Cotton Mather, like Browne in his testimony at Bury St. Edmunds, believed that the Devil could "stir up and excite humors," especially in children and females. Describing the afflictions of Mercy Short, whose possession occurred within a year after the Salem trials, Cotton Mather wrote *Another Brand Pluckt Out of the Burning*. Emulating Browne's testimony, Cotton Mather wrote:

> That the Evil Angels do often take Advantage from Natural Distempers in the Children of Men to annoy them with such further Mischiefs as we call preternatural. The Malignant Vapours and Humours of our Diseased Bodies may be used by Devils, thereinto insinuating as engine of the Execution of their Malice upon those Bodies; and perhaps for this reason one Sex may suffer more Troubles of the kinds from the Invisible World than the other, as well as for that reason for which the Old Serpent made where he did his first Address.[230]

Unfortunately, in terms of what soon would unfold at Salem, Hale's judgment and Browne's opinions continued to influence events even after their deaths. Though witchcraft beliefs were dying out, the impact of Bury St. Edmunds remained. As historian James Sharpe has written, "The Bury St Edmunds trial of 1662 demonstrated how, even in the face of a court willing to entertain the possibility of deception, and anxious to subject a witchcraft accusation to as many of the known tests and methods of proving witchcraft as possible, the accepted standards of proofs in witchcraft trials were still difficult to reject."[231]

The Foreshadowing of Salem: The Goodwin Children & A Hanging in Boston

English colonists arriving in America predictably brought over their fundamental beliefs and traditions concerning witchcraft. They codified their new laws based upon biblical and English precedents, specifically Parliament's 1604 statute.[232] The colonists at Plymouth made witchcraft a capital crime in their "Laws of the Colony" of 1636.[233] One clause in the General Lawes and Libertyes Concerning the Inhabitants of the Massachusetts (1641, repealed 1684) included the biblical injunction, "If any man or woman be a Witch, (that is, hath or consulteth with a familiar spirit) they shall be put to death."[234] By 1672, similar statutes were written into law in Rhode Island and Providence Plantations (1647), New Haven Colony (1656), Connecticut (1672).[235]

Between 1647 and 1663, the New England colonists executed at least fifteen people for witchcraft.[236] The earliest execution occurred in Connecticut on May 26, 1647 when Alse Young was hanged. All that is known about the event is the name, date, and crime. The first instance in which accusations expanded into a witch-hunt in colonial America occurred at Hartford, Connecticut in 1662-3. Here the authorities ordered the execution of at least three, possibly four individuals, based on the accusations of a possessed woman, Ann Cole, and the testimony of a confessed witch, Rebecca Greensmith.[237] After 1663, as in England, it became difficult in the colonies to obtain a conviction for witchcraft. In fact, the next execution for witchcraft in New

England did not occur until 1688, when the widow Glover hanged for bewitching the Goodwin children.[238]

We know about the possession of the Goodwin children chiefly from Reverend Cotton Mather, the son of the famous Reverend Increase Mather. In 1689, he published *Memorable Providences, Relating to Witchcrafts and Possessions*. Similar to his father's *Remarkable Providences*, published five years earlier, it was a collection of stories that promoted the belief that the Devil was in this world and described what had to be done, with God's grace, to defeat him. These popular works influenced opinions throughout the Bay Colony.

The first of Mather's examples of "providences" involved the children of Boston mason John Goodwin, who began suffering unexplainable and terrifying afflictions in the mid-summer of 1688. Bostonians believed the Goodwin children when they accused their neighbor, the poor and elderly widow Glover of witchcraft. Several months later, on November 16, 1688, Glover was hanged on Boston Common.

Like many witchcraft cases, the conflict began with a domestic dispute. The eldest Goodwin child, Martha, thirteen years old, accused the washerwoman of stealing laundry. The washerwoman's mother verbally abused Martha and cursed her. During the early modern period, curses inspired fear, especially from a reputed witch. Their angry mumblings were considered effective threats of forthcoming maleficium.[239] Curses from a rumored witch and the ensuing accusations of witchcraft played an important part in the earlier Glover/Jackson case. As mentioned previously, both the suspected witch and the unfortunate accursed individual could believe in the effectiveness of the curse.[240] As Mather wrote, "…immediately upon which, the poor child became variously indisposed in her health, and visited with strange Fits, beyond those that attend an Epilepsy or a Catalepsy, or those that they call The Diseases of Astonishment."[241]

The afflictions soon spread to three other siblings: John, eleven; Mercy, seven; and Benjamin, five. All four, "…were handled in so sad and strange a manner, as has given matter of Discourse and Wonder to all the Countrey, and of History not unworthy to be considered by more than all the serious or the curious Readers in this New-English World."[242] By early fall, several physicians, including Dr. Thomas Oakes, who Mather considered a "worthy and prudent friend," diagnosed witchcraft.[243] Mather vividly described how the children suffered similar horrific and excruciating troubles simultaneously:

> Sometimes they would be Deaf, sometimes Dumb, and sometimes Blind, and often, all this at once. One while their Tongues would be drawn down their Throats; another-while they would be pull'd out upon their Chins, to a prodigious length. They would have their Mouths opened unto such a Wideness, that their Jaws went out of joint; and anon they would clap together again with a Force like that of a strong Spring-Lock. The same would happen to their Shoulder-Blades, and their Elbows, and Hand-wrists, and several of their joints. They would at times lye in a benumbed condition and be drawn together as those that are ty'd Neck and Heels; and presently be stretched out, yea, drawn Backwards, to such a degree that it was fear'd the very skin of their Bellies would have crack'd. They would make most pitteous out-cries, that they were cut with Knives, and struck with Blows that they could not bear. Their Necks would be broken, so that their Neck-bone would seem dissolved unto them that felt after it; and yet on the sudden, it would become, again so stiff that there was no stirring of their Heads; yea, their Heads would be twisted almost round; and if main Force at any time obstructed a dangerous motion which they seem'd to be upon, they would roar exceedingly. Thus they lay some weeks most pittiful Spectacles; and this while as a further Demonstration of Witchcraft in these horrid Effects, when I went to Prayer by one of them, that was very desireous to hear what I said, the Child utterly lost her Hearing till our Prayer was over.[244]

Like the Throckmorton girls, Mary Glover, and several of the afflicted girls at Salem, the Goodwin children lived in a religious household. According to Mather, the children had "...an observable affection unto divine and sacred things...wherein it was perfectly impossible for any dissimulation of theirs to produce what scores of spectators were amazed at."[245] The Goodwin parents asked five ministers, the Reverends Allen, Moody, Willard, Morton, and Cotton Mather to hold a day of prayer and fasting at their household, which apparently cured the youngest child.[246] The other children, however, continued to be terribly afflicted.

John Goodwin complained about Glover to the Boston magistrates, unnamed by Mather, who questioned her. Apart from Mather's description of her as a hag, a vile woman, a witch, miserable old woman, and an "ignorant and scandalous old woman," we learn only that she was an Irish Roman Catholic washerwoman.[247] The widow Glover presented an unsympathetic and uncooperative figure to the Puritan judges. Speaking through an interpreter, when asked if she believed in God, according to Mather, "…her answer was too blasphemous and horrible for any pen of mine to mention."[248] When she could not properly recite the Lord's Prayer, even with each line carefully repeated to her, the magistrates decided to imprison her.[249] A search of her house turned up puppets, which Glover admitted stroking with her own spittle to torment people. To test this display of witchcraft, the magistrates had the children brought before her:

> …and the Woman still kept stooping and shrinking as one that was almost prest to Death with a mighty Weight upon her. But one of the Images being brought unto her, immediately she started up after an odd manner, and took it into her hand; but she had no sooner taken it, than one of the Children fell into sad Fits, before the whole Assembly.[250]

Upon repetition of the experiment, the same result occurred. At this point, Glover began a lengthy confession. She admitted to being a witch and meeting with Satan. Five or six doctors examined her to see if she "…had not procured to her self by Folly and Madness the Reputation of a Witch."[251] Once the doctors agreed she was of sound mind, the authorities ordered Glover's execution.[252]

At her hanging, Glover told the crowd other witches were involved with afflicting the Goodwin children, so that her own death would bring them no peace. This prophesy turned out to be true as the children remained afflicted.[253] Though Mather was privy to the names of these other possible witches, he kept them to himself.[254]

Mather decided to take Martha Goodwin into his own parsonage. For nearly two months, she provided numerous spectacular displays of possession:

> Variety of Tortures now siez'd upon the Girl; in which besides the forementioned Ails returning upon her, she often would cough up a Ball as big as a small Egg, into the side of her Wind-pipe, that would near choak her…In her ludicrous Fits, one while she would be for Flying; and she would be carried hither and thither, tho not long from the ground, yet so long as to exceed the ordinary power of Nature in our Opinion of it…[255]

Mather attempted to cure her through prayer and scripture. He found that when, "she went to read the Bible her Eyes would be strangely twisted and blinded, and her Neck presently broken, but also that if any one else did read the Bible in the Room, tho it were wholly out of her sight, and without the least voice or noise of it, she would be cast into very terrible Agonies."[256] This happened with several other books, including his father's account of the Ann Cole possession in *Remarkable Providences* and Reverend Samuel Willard's *Treatise of Justification*.[257] It did not happen with Quaker or "popish" books.[258]

An invisible horse, along with a company of unseen demons, appeared to Martha. She rode the horse and spoke with the demons. Like the Throckmorton girls at Warboys, the demons informed her about her fits. Mather relates:

> When I came in, I found her mounted after her fashion, upon her Aerial Steed; which carried her Fancy to the Journeys end. There (or rather then) she maintained a considerable Discourse with Her Company, Listening very attentively when she had propounded any Question, and receiving the Answers with impressions made upon her mind. She said; "Well what do you say? How many Fits more am I to have?—pray, can ye tell how long it shall be before you are hang'd for what you have done?—You are filthy Witches to my knowledge...[259]

About November 27, 1692 (one of the few dates Mather mentioned), two weeks after the hanging of Glover, several ministers, including Reverend Willard, gathered at the Goodwin's home for a day of prayer. Though the children were as afflicted as ever, Mather states this event broke "the power of the enemy."[260]

Though the afflictions subsided, they did not cease completely. Martha Goodwin stayed at Mather's house throughout the winter of 1688-9. Troubling incidents still occurred. When Mather had prayers said for Martha, "...she would be laid as one asleep; but when Prayer was begun, the Devils would still throw her on the Floor, at the feet of him that prayed for her. There she would lye and Whistle and sing and roar, to drown the voice of the Prayer..."[261] Following that, she would violently strike out with her feet and fists. Then, before the end of the prayer, "...she would be laid for Dead, wholly senseless and (unless to a severe Trial) breathless; with her belly swelled like a Drum, and sometimes with croaking Noises in it."[262]

Though Mather provided no dates, a cured Martha probably returned home in the spring of 1689. John Goodwin, aged twelve by then, suffered a relapse, but all appeared well by the time Mather completed *Memorable Providences*, in June 1689.[263] *Memorable Providences*, which dramatically depicted the possessions, undoubtedly influenced many who were present at the Salem witch trials three years later.

Mather hoped his tour de force of supernatural "wonders" and "providences" would establish, beyond any doubt, the existence and terrifying power of witches.[264] Although it is impossible to know precisely what the youthful accusers at Salem knew about previous trials, many of the girls' mannerisms proved remarkably similar to those of the Goodwin children. One of the ministers present at the Salem trials, John Hale noted this. Hale wrote that the girls at Salem were, "…in all things afflicted as bad as John Goodwin's children at Boston, in the year 1689. So that he that will read Mr. Mather's Book of Memorable Providences, page 3 etc., may Read part of what these Children, and afterward sundry grown persons suffered by the hand of Satan, at Salem Village, and parts adjacent."[265]

Not only did this experience resonate throughout the colonial community by way of his book, but also it affected Mather on a personal level. This experience solidified his deeply held belief in witchcraft, which subsequently came into play at Salem. He decided, "…after this, never to use but just one grain of patience with any man that shall go to impose upon me a Denial of Devils, or of Witches."[266]

Modern authors have interpreted the afflictions experienced by the Goodwin children in several ways. Describing the antics of Martha Goodwin, the historian Ola Elizabeth Winslow writes, "Read today, against a heritage of disbelief in witches, they reveal on every page the adroit cleverness of this child, her flattery of Cotton Mather, and his (to us) amazing blindness not to detect her trickery, while his pen was in his hand."[267] Frances Hill, in her *A Delusion of Satan*, sees the possessions differently:

> There can be no doubt that what beset the Goodwin children, Elizabeth Knapp, and all the others described by the Mathers, was clinical hysteria. To read Freud and Breuer's *Studies on Hysteria*, written two centuries later, after reading *Remarkable Providences* and *Memorable Providences*, is to experience déjà vu. The extraordinary body postures, inexplicable pains, deafness, dumbness, and blindness, meaningless babbling, refusal to eat, destructive and self-destructive behavior, always with warnings so no one got hurt, are just the same in all three accounts. So are the exhibitionism, the self-control even in apparent abandonment, and the complete power over parents, caregivers, and everyone else within range.[268]

Chadwick Hansen drew upon the contemporary witchcraft beliefs demonstrated in the Goodwin case to promote his theory that genuine witches existed in New England. The same "society which believes in witchcraft," along with several of the main participants, would be present at Salem. Hanson wrote:

> There has never been a more clear-cut case of witchcraft...what is most important is that her witchcraft plainly worked, and in no indiscriminate fashion. When she tormented one of her dolls, one of the Goodwin children "fell into sad fits." When it is remembered that in a society which believes in witchcraft the violent hysterical symptoms to which the Goodwin children were subject not infrequently terminate in death, it cannot be said that the Boston court acted either harshly or unjustly.[269]

The Glover case clearly affected opinions at Salem four years later. In New England witchcraft cases, possession itself rarely played a prominent part. The last execution for possession-related witchcraft, other than the widow Glover, occurred at Hartford thirty years before Salem. It would appear possession cases, until that of the Goodwin children, were dying out. Mather included a few cases in his *Memorable Providences*, two of which occurred in Connecticut, one involving an unnamed boy in Tocutt (probably between 1644-1677) and another with an unnamed girl in Norwich (1684 or slightly earlier), along with the interesting case of Elizabeth Knapp.[270] The dramatic possession of the Goodwin children, and the publication of the events by a highly respected member of the Puritan clergy, helped create an environment that made the Salem witch trials possible.

Salem: The Self-Destruction of a New England Community by Possession and Panic

This paper has examined several possession-related witchcraft cases that took place before Salem to identify and explore the behaviors and ideas that shaped them. In most of these case studies, there is little evidence that provides personal information or describes the background of the possessed or the accused witches. The abundant documentation surrounding the witch trials at Salem, however, greatly advances our examination of the troubled social dynamics, religious mindset, and personal animus that created such a unique and shocking episode.

The common oversimplification of the Salem witch persecutions of 1692 was that hysterical young girls and an intolerant Puritan ministry caused a widespread witch panic. Superstitious and frightened townspeople turned against one another to combat an outside evil, only to realize later their own culpability. In this scenario, young female accusers initiated and drove the debacle. Zealous and power-hungry clergy promoted fear to maintain their fading power.

This interpretation has undergone drastic revisions in recent years, as historians have presented numerous alternative theories to explain the tragedy at Salem. Some believe that the girls were rebelling against their strict Puritan upbringing and their station in life.[271] Medical explanations for the girls' afflictions include ergot poisoning, hysteria, and encephalitis.[272] Other approaches suggest that social and economic rivalry between powerful families in Salem Village caused the accusations.[273] The historian Chadwick Hanson argued that at least some of the accused actively practiced witchcraft.[274]

The real explanation of "Why Salem" is both multi-causal and elusive. No single theory can account for the bizarre and frightening behavior of a few young girls and the violent reaction of the community. Though this chapter does not provide a comprehensive examination of these theories, it can illustrate the cultural environment and describe specific examples of how the trials progressed due to the community's understanding of witchcraft.

The background of the case is well known. In the winter of 1691-2, the nine-year-old daughter of the Reverend Samuel Parris, Betty, began acting strangely. She screamed and babbled senselessly, refused to do her chores and experienced trances. Her eleven-year-old cousin Abigail also began to act oddly. They barked and howled, ran around the room and hid under furniture. When Parris prayed with them, the girls experienced violent convulsions. On one occasion, Betty threw a Bible across the room, and on another, Abigail threw burning wood from the fireplace.

At first, following a pattern we have seen in previous bewitchment cases, Reverend Parris believed that the girls' strange behavior had natural causes. Ministers from nearby towns gathered to pray and fast at his parsonage. A doctor, usually identified as Dr. Griggs, having failed to find any natural explanation for their behavior, diagnosed the children as being under the "evil hand." This reliance upon the supernatural was perfectly consistent with both religious and medical thinking of the time.[275]

The afflictions, however, quickly spread to Parris' neighbors. By late February 1692, Ann Putnam Jr., Elizabeth Hubbard, Mercy Lewis, and Mary Walcott, all between the ages of twelve to nineteen, also became afflicted.[276] Ann Putnam's mother, Ann Sr., became the first adult to suffer similar symptoms, giving the witchcraft idea additional legitimacy. Gossip and fear rapidly spread throughout the community.

With the symptoms spreading, friends and family of the girls pressured them into declaring the source of their torments, and the girls accused Tituba (the Parris' slave from Barbados), Sarah Osborne (a sickly old woman with a questionable reputation), and Sarah Good (a universally disliked beggar) of afflicting them. The families of the afflicted children filed complaints, and the magistrates summoned the women to stand trial.

On March 1, 1692, Justices of the Peace John Hathorne and Jonathan Corwin commenced the preliminary inquest into the guilt of the three women. Though both Hathorne and Corwin were experienced merchants and politicians, neither man was a lawyer.[277] At the time, Massachusetts had no charter, leaving an unusual legal situation. One result of this was although Hathorne and Corwin could examine and commit the accused to prison to await an eventual trial, they could not sentence or convict.[278]

Sarah Good, the first person examined, promptly experienced the girls' dramatic behavior and testimony. The girls acted together to produce a truly terrifying courtroom environment, both at the preliminary hearings and later at the Court of Oyer and Terminer. After Good vigorously denied her guilt, Judge Hathorne enlisted help from the girls. The magistrate's clerk, Ezekiel Cheever wrote that Hathorne "…desired the children, all of them, to look upon her and see if this were the person that had hurt them, and so they all did look upon her and said this was one of the persons that did torment them."[279] In their written summary of the proceedings, Hathorne and Corwin described the children as "…dredfully tortred & tormented for a short space of tyme," and how the girls then leveled the accusations directly at Good.[280] This obvious cooperation and encouragement between Hathorne and Corwin and the accusers continued throughout the trials.

In order to deflect the blame from herself, Good accused Sarah Osborne of afflicting the children. Osborne, whose examination immediately followed Good's, now stood accused by the four girls as well as Good. Mercy Lewis testified that Osborne's specter had told her to write in her book. This referred to the belief that witches signed Satan's book as a contractual obligation to serve him. Osborne replied she was more likely to be bewitched that do the bewitching, but her poor attendance at church service (credibly explained by her ill health) condemned her in the eyes of the judges.

Tituba followed Osborne that same day. As a woman, slave, and accused witch, she understood her dangerous predicament. She proceeded to weave tales that she believed the judges wanted to hear. The ruse worked, and though she confessed to meeting with the Devil, she eventually survived. Her stories were a blend of Caribbean and English witchcraft, which the judges unreservedly believed. She reported that four women and a man afflicted the children. When Hathorne asked for the names, Tituba could only identify Good and Osborne. She stated she flew to injure the children "…upon a stick or pole and Good and Osburn behind me. We ride taking hold of one another; don't know how we go, for I saw no trees nor path but was presently there."[281]

Satan, described by Tituba as a tall, white-haired man from Boston, dressed in black, asked her to help him hurt and murder the children. She added such details as a yellow bird familiar (along with strange other creatures). Upon hearing this, the girls fell into more convulsions, and Hathorne asked Tituba to identify who was hurting them.[282] She blamed Good. For two more days, Tituba continued her eccentric testimony. The spectators hung on every word. From now on, some of the most intelligent and respected people in Massachusetts, influenced by the frightened imagination of a slave from Barbados, tragically allowed the executions of innocent people.

Since these three women conformed to the conventional stereotype of witches, the judges had no difficulty in deciding to hold them. On March 7, they traveled to the jail in Boston. Prison, however, could be a death sentence in itself. Shortly after her incarceration, Sarah Good gave birth (the infant soon died in jail). On May 10, after two months in jail, the ailing Sarah Osborne also died.[283]

On March 11, at Parris' parsonage, ministers gathered to pray and fast. The children again began to act strangely, and one suffered a "convulsion Fit, her Limbs being twisted several ways, and very stiff, but presently her fit would be over."[284] That same day, another spectre appeared to Ann Putnam Jr. Ann alleged Martha Corey, a respected but opinionated Church member, had appeared to her.

Corey had been disdainful of the proceedings, and told people so. She was aware her name might come up, and when approached on March 12 by Edward Putnam (Anne's uncle) and Ezekiel Cheever, Martha continued her mocking approach. She told them, "I know what you are come for you are come to talke with me about being a witch, but I am none."[285] This appeared to the two men as a supernatural ability to read their minds, and Martha cryptically added, "Does shee tell you what clothes I have on?"[286] Though Martha intended this to defray the gravity of the men's supposedly secret purpose, it instead provided confirmation to their suspicions that she was a witch.

On March 21, 1692, Martha Corey, a member of Parris' Salem Village church, was the next person examined.[287] The girls, sitting together in the front, dramatically fell into their fits, screaming that Corey was biting, pinching, and strangling them. They also said she kept a yellow bird as her familiar. According to the Reverend Lawson, the author of the earliest published account of the trials in his *A Brief and True Narrative* (1692), Corey testified:

> …they were poor, distracted, Children, and no heed to be given to what they said. Mr. Hathorne and Mr. Noyes replyed, it was the judgment of all that were present, they were Bewitched, and only she, the Accused Person said, they were distracted. It was observed several times, that if she did but bite her Under lip in time of Examination the persons afflicted were bitten on their armes and wrists and produced the Marks before the Magistrates, Ministers and others. And being watched for that, if she did but Pinch her

> Fingers, or Graspe one hand hard in another, they were Pinched and produced the Marks before the Magistrates, and Spectators…After these postures were watched, if said C. did but stir her feet, they were afflicted in their Feet, and stamped fearfully.[288]

On March 21, Corey was sent to prison, followed a two days later by Sarah Good's daughter, Dorcas. Jailed for nine months, and locked up with smaller, but heavy, chains, Dorcas never psychologically recovered.

The following day, March 24, Rebecca Nurse, a widely respected and a covenanted member of the Salem Town church,[289] faced the same treatment. Seventy-one years old, ill, and hard of hearing, in a crowded and noisy courtroom, Rebecca confronted her accusers. As Hathorne questioned her, the girls continued their fits and mimicked Nurse's gestures. Reverend Lawson wrote that Nurse's movements:

> …did produce like effects as to, Biteing, Pinching, Bruising, Tormenting, at their Breasts, by her Leaning, and when, bended Back, were as if their Backs was broken. The afflicted persons said, the Black Man, whispered to her in the Assembly, and therefore she could not hear what the Magistrates said unto her…. Others also were there grievously afflicted, so there was once such an hideous scietch and noise, (which I heard as I walked, at a little distance from the Meeting house,) as did amaze me, and some that were within, told me the whole assembly was struck with consternation, and they were afraid, that those that sate next to them, were under the influence of Witchcraft.[290]

This kind of courtroom drama, combined with depositions given by Elizabeth Hubbard, Mary Walcott, Ann Putnam Sr. and Jr. describing their torment from Nurse's "apperishtion," left Rebecca Nurse bewildered and angry. She was also distressed over the influence her accusers possessed, as the judges appeared to believe them and not her. Samuel Parris had difficulty taking notes due to the commotion. He ends his transcript with "This is a true account of the sume of her examination but by reason of great noyses by the afflicted & many speakers, many things are pretermitted." The last thing Nurse said in Parris' transcript was that "I cannot help it, the Devil may appear in my shape."[291] The ordeal so shook Rebecca that her husband had to carry her from the meetinghouse. Shortly afterwards, she was taken to prison.

The jailing of Rebecca Nurse, with her reputation for exceptional piety, created a disturbing shift in the dynamics of the trial. A climate of trepidation permeated Salem as individuals became more apprehensive about their neighbors. Without strong safeguards on the type of evidence allowed, and fear in the air, the prisons soon began to fill up.

Unfortunately, this panic spread to other towns, even those that did not share some of Salem's unique troubles. By May, residents of Billerica, Andover, Marblehead, Lynn, Reading, Charleston, Topsfield, Gloucester, Malden, and Beverly had accused each other of witchcraft.[292] In June, the constable of Andover, Joseph Ballard brought Ann Putnam, Jr. and Mary Walcott to town to uncover possible witches. Blindfolded, the two girls touched several men and women, identifying four of them as witches. After the girls left, the townspeople accused an additional thirty-seven of their neighbors.[293]

Other upstanding members of the Salem community found themselves in front of the magistrates as a result of the girls' accusations. Soon, the Court imprisoned Giles Corey, John and Elizabeth Proctor, Mary Easty and Sarah Cloyce (Rebecca Nurse's sisters), and Elizabeth Cary (the wife of a wealthy shipbuilder). Sheriffs ignominiously bought back Salem's former minister, George Burroughs, from Maine under arrest. As the court had no authority to sentence or execute, only imprison, the jails continued to fill.

With the girls experiencing convulsions during the examinations in front of the accused and the magistrates, Hathorne and Corwin decided to allow a wide assortment of evidence. Throughout these preliminary examinations, lasting from March through May, 1692, they had several women stripped and searched for a "witch's teat" (any skin abnormality, such as a scar or a birthmark, which could be considered the site where the witch's familiar suckled). The Court also accepted the touch test, based on the belief that having the afflicted person touch the accused witch could alleviate the affliction.

Other tests included having witches attempt to flawlessly recite passages from the Bible (real witches were believed to be unable to do so) and accepting testimony from other villagers about misfortunes occurring after arguments with the accused (though it may have transpired decades earlier). All these tests and procedures performed at Salem had been used in previous trials concerning possession, though they were rapidly losing favor among English jurists.

The most controversial evidence accepted was "spectral evidence." This centered on the belief that witches could send out their "specters" to afflict people. This raised the theological/legal issue of whether God allowed the Devil to send out specters in the shape of innocent, even virtuous, people. The magistrates, however, believed God would not allow the Devil to implicate pious people, and determined spectral evidence to be valid. One of the many examples of this occurred at the trial of Rebecca Nurse, when Ann Putnam Jr. deposed:

> I saw the Apperishtion of gooddy Nurs: and she did inmediatly afflect me…she hath greviously afflicted me by biting pinching and pricking me: urging me to writ in hir book and also on the 24th of march being the day of hir examination I was greviously tortured by hir dureing the time of hir examination and also severall times sence and also dureing the time of hir examination I saw the Apperishtion of Rebekah nurs goe and hurt the bodys of Misry lewes mary wolcott Elizabeth Hubbrd and Abigail Williams.[294]

Apart from accepting the controversial evidence, the judges encouraged the accusers to cooperate as a team; no one thought to separate them to check the consistency and reliability of their stories. The Reverend Deodat Lawson, a former minister of Salem Village, wrote the earliest account of trials in his *A Brief and True Narrative* (1692). Describing their collaboration, he wrote:

> They did in the Assembly mutually Cure each other, even with a Touch of their Hand, when Strangled, and otherwise Tortured; and would endeavor to get to their Afflicted, to Relieve them…They did also foretell when another's Fit was a-coming, and would say, "Look to her! She will have a Fit presently," which fell out accordingly, as many can bear witness, that heard and saw it.[295]

With the prosecutorial zeal of the judges and the lack of a defense attorney, this gave a great advantage to the plaintiffs.[296] The girls' dramatics, the chaos of the courtroom, and the spectators' beliefs concerning witchcraft made the defense of the accused even harder.

Fortunately, on May 14, 1692, Reverend Increase Mather returned from London, bringing with him both a new charter and a new royal governor, Sir William Phips. Mather had sailed to England in April 1688 to negotiate a new charter, which he hoped would allow Massachusetts to retain its system of self-government. He failed to achieve this goal, however, and the new charter contained provisions that weakened the authority of the Puritan political theocracy. Not only would King William now choose the governor of the colony, but the electorate would now be broadened to include non-covenanted church members.[297] Though Massachusetts lost some of it most fundamental and important rights, Mather felt he had negotiated the best arrangement possible.[298]

Phips, who made a name for himself as a military commander and a discoverer of sunken treasure, had been born in what is now Maine.[299] Neither man knew of the panic enveloping Massachusetts until they arrived. By the time Mather and Governor Phips returned, the magistrates at Salem had already imprisoned forty-two people for witchcraft.[300] Describing his predicament in a letter to the clerk of the Privy Council in London, October 12, 1692, Phips wrote:

> When I first arrived I found this Province miserably harassed with a most Horrible witchcraft or Possession of Devils which had broke in upon several Towns, some scores of poor people were taken with

preternatural torments some scalded with brimstone, some had pins stuck in their flesh others hurried into the fire and water and some dragged out of their houses and carried over the tops of trees for many Miles together...The loud cries and clamors of the friends of the afflicted people with the advice of the Deputy Governor and many others prevailed with me to give a Commission of Oyer and Terminer for discovering what witchcraft might be at the bottom or whether it were not a possession.[301]

The men Phips chose for this new Court of Oyer and Terminer were prominent citizens; in fact, they all belonged to the Governor's Council. The chief judge was William Stoughton, who became acting governor in August and September when Phips was in Maine with the army.[302] Stoughton also succeeded Phips as governor of the colony. Hathorne and Corwin found themselves discharged.

Before the trials began, Judge John Richards had asked the Reverend Cotton Mather for his views. Though Mather firmly believed in witchcraft, he was concerned about the reliance upon spectral evidence. Mather replied in a letter dated May 31:

...do not lay more stress upon pure Specter testimony than it will bear...If upon the bare supposal of a poor creature's being represented by a Specter, too great a progress be made by the Authority in ruining a poor neighbor so represented, it may be that a door may be thereby opened for the Devils to obtain from the Courts in the invisible world a license to proceed unto most hideous desolations upon the repute & repose of such as have yet been Kept from the great transgression. If mankind have thus far once consented unto the credit of Diabolical representations the Door is opened![303]

The Court of Oyer and Terminer convened on June 2, 1692. By this time, approximately seventy people had been accused, with no end in sight.[304] Bridget Bishop, without powerful friends, was the initial defendant. At her trial, the girls fell into fits. They stated that Bishop's specter had bitten, pinched, and choked them. The girls collapsed to the floor when Bishop looked at them and revived when she touched them. Workers had found dolls and pins in the walls of Bishop's home, a damning sign of witchcraft. Other spectral evidence, along with assorted rumors and Bishop's wicked reputation doomed her.

On June 10, 1692, Bridget Bishop was hanged. This event created a small rift in the community. Richard Saltonstall, the only member of the court with a legal education, quit the court in disgust. Unsure about the predominant use of spectral evidence, Governor Phips turned to the area's ministers for guidance.

The ministers responded to Phips' request on June 15 with "The Return of several Ministers consulted by his excellency, and the Honorable Council, upon the present Witchcrafts in Salem Village." After thanking the magistrates for detecting the witchcraft, the ministers advised strict caution concerning spectral evidence:

> We judge that in the prosecution of these, and all such Witchcrafts, there is need of a very critical and exquisite Caution, lest by too much Credulity for things received only upon the Devil's Authority, there be a Door opened for a long Train of miserable Consequences, and Satan get an advantage over us, for we should not be ignorant of his Devices…Presumptions whereupon Persons may be committed, and much more Convictions, whereupon Persons may be condemned as guilty of Witchcrafts, ought certainly to be more considerable, than barely the accused Person being represented by a Specter unto the Afflicted; inasmuch as 'tis an undoubted and a notorious thing that a Demon may, by God's Permission, appear even to ill purposes, in the Shape of an innocent, yea, and a virtuous man: Nor can we esteem Alterations made in the Sufferers, by a Look or Touch of the Acused to be an infallible Evidence of Guilt; but frequently liable to be abused by the Devil's Legerdemains.[305]

These were not new concerns. At their inquests, both Rebecca Nurse and Martha Cory stated the Devil could take whatever shape he wanted. During his defense, the Reverend George Burroughs stated witches could not "…Torment other people at a distance."[306] This boiled down to a theological/judicial conflict over the interpretation of demonic possession and the power of Satan. Now powerful and well-respected ministers began to disagree with the Court's unyielding stance. If Satan could send out specters in the form of the innocent for his own evil purposes, the whole edifice of the indisputability of spectral evidence would collapse.

Defying explanation, not only did the trials continue, but the Court abandoned caution. It achieved a one hundred percent conviction rate; the Court found none of the accused innocent. The magistrates ignored petitions signed by many members of the community attesting to the innocence and propriety of some of the accused, such as Rebecca Nurse and the Proctors. They chose to ignore the advice of the increasingly concerned ministers. They also judged some of the most powerful people in the state on such questionable evidence. John Alden, the Englishes, and the Carys eventually fled, leaving much of their possessions but possibly saving their lives.[307] Phips, Saltonstall, and most of the region's ministers told the Court to use spectral evidence cautiously and only with other, more tangible, evidence.[308] The Court, however, believed God would not allow the Devil to implicate pious people, and determined spectral evidence to be valid. It accepted the hysterical accusations and formulaic depositions as gospel truth.

There are numerous examples of the Court's problematical application of their authority. Judge Stoughton sent back the jury that exonerated Rebecca Nurse to reconsider their finding. Apart from having a admirable reputation, Nurse's daughter, Sarah, had seen Goody Bibber stick herself with own pins at the trial, crying out Rebecca Nurse had pinched her[309] (presumably, by the use of her spectre). The jury dutifully returned with a verdict of guilty. According to contemporary writer Robert Calef, during Sarah Good's trial, an accuser showed part of a knife that purportedly Good had used to assault her. A young man immediately produced the remainder of the blade, stating he had thrown the piece from his broken knife in front of the accuser the day before. The accuser "…was bidden by the Court not to tell lyes; and was improved (after as she had been before) to give Evidence against the Prisoners."[310]

Though "cried out upon" several times, Jonathan Corwin's mother-in-law, Margaret Thatcher (possibly the wealthiest woman in the country) escaped questioning altogether.[311] The judges also dissuaded the girls from accusing Reverend Samuel Willard.

The court disregarded the recanting of false and forced confessions. Many confessed simply to save their lives. This is particularly tragic in the case of George Jacobs Sr. and his granddaughter, Margaret Jacobs. Arrested on the May 10, 1692, Margaret accused her grandfather while he avowed his innocence. On August 5, guilty verdicts arrived for George Jacobs and Reverend Burroughs. From jail, Margaret courageously recanted her accusations against both men. They hanged on August 19. She remained jailed until early December.[312] In another case, Sarah Churchill told Sarah Ingersoll she had lied and wanted to take back her accusation. When Ingersoll appealed for her to do so, Churchill replied she could not, as she had been threatened with imprisonment by the judges if she did.[313]

Many in the community, however, rejected the Court's use of spectral evidence and accusations from confessed witches. By early October, with the jails overflowing and the accusations and confessions continuing, Increase Mather passed around a manuscript version of a soon to be published book entitled *Cases of Conscience Concerning Evil Spirits Personating Men* (1693). Of the Court's acceptance of the girls' accusations, Mather wrote, "If all these things concur in the persons concerning whom the Question is, we may conclude them to be *Daemoniacks*. And if so, no *Juror* can with a safe Conscience look on the Testimony of such, as sufficient to take away the Life of any man."[314]

On October 29, 1692, Phips dissolved the Court of Oyer and Terminer. He set up a new Superior Court of Judicature to retry the jailed. Thomas Danforth (a critic of the trials who had been succeeded by Stoughton as Deputy Governor) replaced Corwin.[315] Stoughton remained in charge. Spectral evidence became inadmissible.[316] By abandoning this significant part of the accusations, the indictments collapsed. This new court convicted only three out of fifty-six people indicted, and Phips subsequently pardoned them.

Phips needed to explain both the events and justify his decisions to London. Though blaming Stoughton for the deaths and excesses served his own self-interest, Phip's opinion makes sense. He reasoned he was away combating the French and Indians when the trials occurred. Phips, in his interpretation of the events following his return, wrote on February 21, 1693:

> ...but when I returned I found people much dissatisfied at the proceedings of the Court, for about Twenty persons were condemned and executed of which number some were thought by many persons to be innocent. The Court still proceeded in the same method of trying them, which was by the evidence of the afflicted persons who when they were brought into the Court as soon as the suspected witches looked upon them instantly fell to the ground in strange agonies and grievous torments, but when touched by them upon the arm or some other part of their flesh they immediately revived and came to themselves, upon [which] they made oath that the Prisoner at the Bar did afflict them and that they saw their shape or specter come from their bodies which put them to such pains and torments...but at length I found that the Devil did take upon him the shape of Innocent persons and some were accused of whose innocency I was well assured...The Deputy Govr. notwithstanding persisted vigorously in the same method, to the great dissatisfaction and disturbance of the people, until I put an end to the Court and stopped the proceedings, which I did because I saw many innocent persons might otherwise perish...[317]

The legally sanctioned hysteria, suspicion, and conflicts of the Salem witchcraft trials were over. The process of recovery and forgiveness for the community began, along with the difficulty of understanding why the trials occurred in the first place.

We have seen how events at Salem at first resembled earlier possession cases. The girls had convulsions, made strange vocalizations, expressed abhorrence of the word of God, and fell into trances. The response of parents and neighbors was prayer, fasting, and consultation of doctors. They did not consider witchcraft responsible at first, nor did they take the law into their own hands. As was true in England, laws pertaining to witchcraft not only existed, but magistrates had recently enforced them in Boston at the trial and execution of the widow Glover.[318] Unlike the earlier cases, however, the hysteria at Salem spread beyond siblings into the community at large. The number of accused witches was also much greater. The girls' allegations spread to people they had never met as well as the colony's elite.

If the Salem community had been secure and harmonious, there is every reason to believe that perhaps a few hangings would have taken place, but no panic would have ensued. This was not the case. Salem at this time experienced certain severe difficulties, both internally and externally, which exacerbated the tension brought about by the witchcraft accusations. The way the trials turned out the way they did must be seen through the filter of these assorted mindsets, folk beliefs, tensions, and conflicts.[319]

Politically, the English Parliament revoked Massachusetts' charter in 1688, leaving the colony bereft of a governor and without a legitimate legal and administrative system until 1692. When Increase Mather returned with the new chapter, it was apparent that Massachusetts had lost several fundamental rights. The charter officially ended the Puritan-dominated world envisioned by John Winthrop.[320] Though it alleviated the colony's political and legal uncertainty, it also decisively demonstrated the changes taking place in Puritan society.

Spiritually, in colonial Massachusetts, the reality of witchcraft was an accepted fact of life. Salem's Puritan inhabitants lived in a world based upon a spiritual vision that each difficulty experienced, personally and for the colony, illustrated God's ultimate design and purpose. The Puritan clergy elucidated this vision, as well as helped the community and magistrates to form perceptions about witchcraft. To illustrate instances in which God had played a role in the lives of individuals,

Reverends Increase and Cotton Mather recorded their astonishing "providences" and "wonders" for the edification of the public. Increase published *Remarkable Providences* in 1684, his son Cotton followed with *Memorable Providences Relating to Witchcraft and Possession* in 1689.

The Mathers' books contained an assortment of purportedly true stories concerning sea-deliverances, comets, lightning, apparitions, demons, witchcraft and witch trials, captivity stories, and other unusual events, which were meant to buttress the belief in God and the invisible world. It also included stories about the "…most Remarkable Judgments of God upon Sinners," which derided drunkards and Quakers.[321] These popular volumes influenced perceptions about the reality and danger of witchcraft, though no direct evidence exists that they inspired the Salem trial specifically.[322] Unfortunately, this intensely spiritual vision of New England, coupled with some disastrous secular circumstances, did create the environment necessary for the witchcraft trials.

Another source of anxiety was violent Indian attacks, spurred on by their French allies, against the colony and nearby territories.[323] This frightening situation naturally distressed Salem's residents. Indians raided York, only fifty miles from Salem, on January 24, 1692, with over one hundred people captured or killed.[324] Many Puritans viewed the Indians as Satan's minions. Cotton Mather later described the Indians "…to have been horrid *Sorcerers*, and hellish *Conjurers*, and such as Conversed with *Dæmons*."[325]

Geography also divided the community between Salem Town and Salem Village. Salem Town, the colony's second busiest seaport after Boston, was more commercial, urbanized, and prosperous than the Village.[326] The Village, mainly a collection of farms, had been trying to secede from Salem Town since the mid-1660s.[327] Salem Town wanted the taxes and obligations from the inhabitants of Salem Village to continue. For example, men from Salem Village would have to travel several miles away from their families and farms to perform their duties as night watchmen to guard Salem Town. Though Salem Village had its own church, members had to journey to Salem Town to take communion, many times in poor weather.

Two powerful families, the Porters and the Putnams, represented this internal conflict in the Village. Both families acquired supporters, which led to decades of squabbling over the political leadership of their community, as well as seemingly endless litigation between neighbors. The Porters had ties with Salem Town, as their daughters married into the merchant elite while the family as a whole grew more wealthy and powerful. The Putnams lived exclusively in the Village, and strongly promoted the idea of secession. As the fortunes of the Town rose, so did the power and wealth of the Porters, which had eclipsed the Putnams by 1681.[328]

This local factionalism even tainted the religious arena, as both groups attempted to manipulate Salem's ministers to be on their side. Salem's ministers before Reverend Parris, Reverends James Bayley (1672-1680), George Burroughs (1680-1684), and Deodat Lawson (1684-1688), could not reconcile the families or alleviate the dissension in the community. They stayed only a few years, leaving disgruntled and disheartened.[329] Reverend Parris, however, firmly allied himself with the village-based Putnams. Significantly, the accused witches were from Porter's supporters, the accusers from the Putnams and their allies.[330]

The people of Salem desperately needed a healer and conciliator for their community. Parris, however, a failed businessman turned minister, had difficulties from the start. His pecuniary requirements and hard bargaining in his original interviews and contract did not endear him to many. His prickly disposition, demanding attitude, self-righteousness, and inability to work with others, caused some members of the congregation to seek his dismissal. Parris' biased views against his perceived enemies pervaded his sermons and his interpersonal contacts.[331]

During the preliminary hearings of the witches, Parris sided with the Putnam family (both had afflicted children). Present at each examination, he transcribed at least fifteen of them and testified against ten of the accused.[332] Throughout the trials, Parris steadfastly agreed with the magistrates and their decisions. Far from being the mediator Salem needed, Parris was instrumental at helping his community tear itself apart.

An example of this partiality occurred on March 27, 1692, only three days after the examination of Rebecca Nurse, when Parris based his sermon on John 6: 70, "Have not I chosen you twelve, and one of you is a devil." It included phrases such as "There are devils as well as saints in Christ's Church," "Christ Knows who these devils are," "That God would not suffer devils in the guise of saints to associate with us. One sinner destroys much good; how much more one Devil" and "Oh it is a dreadful thing to be a devil, & yet to sit down at the Lord's table."[333] Parris attempted to solidify an unambiguous connection between the devil in the church and covenanted church member Rebecca Nurse.

Viewed as a possession case, the events at Salem began characteristically with two young girls acting strangely, falling into trances, and having fits. Unlike other cases examined, the possessions at Salem ignited terrifying social disorder as a confluence of local tensions and personal animosities combined with a colony-wide anxiety over uncertain religious, political, and security issues. We have seen how the participants of the trials interpreted the possession crisis as both an internal and external attack on the community. They feared consecrated members of their churches were allying themselves with Satan himself to destroy God's plan for New England. By the time the hysteria had ended, and cooler heads decided Satan had deceived them into executing their innocent neighbors, nineteen people had been hanged, five died in prison, and one had been pressed to death by stones.[334]

Conclusion: Common Patterns And Unanswered Questions

As we have seen, the phenomenon of possession presents interesting insights into a culture's religious, political, medical, and legal principles. By focusing on seven specific possession cases that occurred in early modern England and colonial America from 1589 to 1692, we can see how local circumstances, national issues, community relationships, and the impact of individuals influenced and affected instances of possession. From these studies, we can make several generalizations that increase our understanding of various aspects of society in early modern England and colonial Massachusetts.

Before we examine the specific generalizations, it is important to recognize that two of our case studies specifically involve fraud, perpetrated by John Darrell in 1597-99 and Brian Gunter in 1604-06. These two men taught William Somers and Anne Gunter what symptoms to exhibit and whom to accuse. Interestingly enough, both John Darrell and Brian Gunter used *The Most Strange and Admirable Discoverie of the Three Witches of Warboys* pamphlet, which was described in our first case study, for their ideas about what a "genuine" possession should look like. Although these cases involve fraud, they followed the stereotypical characteristics of possession in order to appear genuine. These examples of deception are included in the case studies to demonstrate that "dissembling," or faking possession, all the way to trial, was a real possibility. Even at Salem, for instance, participants in the events accused the girls of faking their symptoms. Martha Carrier testified the accusing girls would dissemble if she looked at them, Mary Warren (herself an accuser) stated these same girls dissembled, and John Alden accused them of playing "juggling tricks, falling down, crying out, and staring in people's faces."[335] Daniel Elliot testified he heard one of the accusing girls brag "...she did it for sport; they must have some sport."[336] Dorcas Hoar called her accusers liars, and threatened "...God will stop the mouths of liars."[337] This uncertainty over the authenticity of the possessions was one reason why trials involved the testing of the accusers as well as the accused.

Our studies of the seven cases demonstrate that the afflictions of the possessed were very similar. In all our case studies, a person or persons between the ages of nine and twenty, usually female, fell ill with unusual symptoms. Though the exact symptoms varied from case to case, they included convulsions, loss of speech, sight, hearing, or appetite, abnormal vocalizations, hallucinations, breathing difficulties, and inexplicable pains. Unlike contemporary cases occurring in France, which usually involved nuns, the afflicted in our case studies displayed virtually no explicit sexual behaviors.

For example, in our first case study, Jane Throckmorton:

> ...would sneeze very loud and thick for the space of half an hour together, and presently as one in a great trance or swoon lay quietly as long; soon after she would begin to swell and heave up her belly so as none was able to bend her or keep her down; sometimes she would shake one leg and no other part of her, as if the palsey had been in it, sometimes the other; presently she would shake one of her arms, and then the other, soon after her head, as if she had been infected with the running palsey."[338]

In the Mary Glover case, Mary's afflictions became much worse in the presence of the accused witch, Elizabeth Jackson. When she saw Jackson, Mary would:

> ...(sometimes) wallow over unto her, other sometimes, rising up in the middle, rebounding wise turne over, unto her, her elbowes being then most deformedly drawn inwards, and withall plucked upwards, to her Chin; but the handes and wrests, turned downwards, and wrethed outward; a position well becoming the malice

Conclusion: Common Patterns And Unanswered Questions

of that efficient [cause]. This tumbling, or casting over towards the witch, when she came to the bedside, or touched her, was at the first two tryalls very palpably playne, and towards her only;...in this fitt, the mouth being fast shut, and her lipps close, there cam a voyce through her nostrills, that sounded very like (especially at some time) Hange her, or Honge her.[339]

In our two fraudulent cases, William Somers' bizarre afflictions led to bestiality with a dog, while Anne Gunter allegedly vomited pins and grew taller and heavier during her fits. The Pacy sisters and Ann Durrant of Lowestoft also vomited pins and suffered extreme convulsions. The painful and terrifying contortions of Goodwin children quickly led to the suspicion of witchcraft. The girls at Salem experienced fits and contortions, but their most significant affliction was claiming they could see, and be harmed by, the specters of the accused. With these spectral visions considered admissible evidence, the jails began to fill. Spectral visions also played a part with the Throckmorton children, the Pacy sisters, and Martha Goodwin.

Another pattern in the majority of the case studies is that the afflicted children or adolescents were under some type of stress that possibly initiated the symptoms. William Somers suffered epileptic-like symptoms he had originally experienced as a boy.[340] At Warboys, the Throckmorton children had just moved into their grandmother's manor only three months earlier when Jane Throckmorton's illness began. It could have been the appearance of a visiting elderly woman bearing the outward characteristics of a witch that frightened nine-year-old Jane enough for her to associate her symptoms with witchcraft. According to the Warboys pamphlet, Jane pointed to Alice Samuel and stated, "Grandmother, look where the old witch sitteth...Did you ever see...one more like a witch than she is?[341] After this exchange, which Alice Samuel had done apparently nothing to provoke, Jane's illness worsened and spread to her sisters.

As for the other case studies, Mary Glover fell ill immediately after a terrifying confrontation with Elizabeth Jackson, in which the elderly woman cursed the fourteen-year-old with "…my daughter shall have clothes when thou art dead and rotten."[342] According to Anne Gunter's confession, when she was ill with symptoms of 'suffocation of the mother,' Brian Gunter threatened, beat, and drugged her in order to revenge himself against his neighbor, Elizabeth Gregory.[343]

Deborah Pacy fell ill immediately after observing an intense argument between her father and a reputed witch. Martha Goodwin, in a scene reminiscent of the Mary Glover/Elizabeth Jackson argument, suffered fits after a suspected witch fiercely cursed at her.

Salem, however, stands as an exception to the other case studies in this regard. Despite the abundance of contemporary material describing the stresses, problems, and fears that sustained and exacerbated the events at Salem (see below), the initial incident that triggered the afflictions of Betty Parris and Abigail Williams is problematical. Before their illnesses, there is no documentation describing any conflicts they had with those they first accused, namely Tituba, Sarah Osborne, and Sarah Good. The traditional narrative, the one found in most works on Salem, depicts Tituba, the Parris' slave, as regaling a small circle of girls and female adolescents with stories of witchcraft and the occult learned from her original home in Barbados.[344] This story appears to be the work of nineteenth century writers, as Bernard Rosenthal observes, "In the enormous quantity of data available for examining the Salem witch trials…in all the contemporary accounts of what happened—not a single person suggests that Tituba told stories of witchcraft or voodoo."[345]

The same lack of primary sources also brings into question the story of this "circle of girls" seeking to foretell their future through magic.[346] According to tradition, after the girls broke an egg into a glass, the shape they egg took would then supposedly symbolize the occupation of the future husband. When the egg took the shape of a coffin, the girls became terrified, which triggered the afflictions, which lead inexorably to the witch trials. This account originally came from Reverend John Hale's *A Modest Enquiry into the Nature of Witchcraft*, published posthumously ten years after the trials.[347] In it, Hale described how an unnamed individual told him that one of the afflicted girls saw a coffin using this egg and glass experiment. According to Hale, the girl never recovered and died without marrying. With so many unsubstantiated accusations in the air in 1692, this one by an unidentified girl hardly seems convincing. Though Hale also wrote he cured a different girl by prayer who performed this type of fortune telling, this still leaves us with only one event that concerned one individual. Apart from the brief mention in Hale's book, there is no other primary source material describing any of the accusing girls of using any method of fortune telling. Several of the accused, however, namely Dorcas Hoar, Sarah Cole, and Samuel Wardwell, were charged with fortune telling.[348]

Personal and family stress, in turn, reflected wider tensions and issues seen in each of our case studies. The arrival of the powerful Throckmortons to Warboys may have upset the balance of community relationships.[349] The trials involving Mary Glover and John Darrell were well-known because of the religious controversy dispossessions provoked. Their cases involved some of the highest-ranking members of the political and religious hierarchy of the day. Brian Gunter's nefarious scheme to have Elizabeth Gregory hanged was the real explanation for his daughter's "afflictions."

The economic tension concerning Lowestoft's suit against Greater Yarmouth, in which Samuel Pacy personally participated in by traveling to London earlier in the year, possibly negatively affected his relationships with his neighbors (such as the impoverished and unpopular Amy Denny) and his family.[350] The political and religious environment of John Goodwin, a "pious and sober" Puritan (according to Cotton Mather), could have been distressed over the revocation of the Massachusetts charter, which occurred in the same year as his children's afflictions.[351]

The numerous problems plaguing Salem Village included the village's lack of legal status, political and religious domination by Salem Town, and the threats from the Indians. Salem Village also experienced feuding between the powerful and interrelated Putnam and the

Porter families, which led to years of bitter lawsuits and the development of factional rivalry. Unfortunately, the Salem Village Church and its ministers became the focal point for this conflict since its earliest years in the mid-1670's. Reverend Parris, a lightning rod for controversy and unpopular with many important people in the Village, only exacerbated these tensions within the community with his prickly and argumentative personality. As many Villagers chose sides and refused to contribute to Parris' salary, Parris in turn used the church pulpit to vent his personal animosities through sermons and carefully chosen scripture readings. With a controversial minister and the community estranged by the Putnam and the Porter conflict, these deep divisions, anger, and fear allowed the accusations to proliferate.

At the outset, in all our cases (apart from the Darrell/Somers case, for which we have no documentation concerning Somers' family), parents did not believe that witchcraft had caused their children's illness. In all our cases, parents consulted a physician in the hope of a cure, but none of the physicians had the slightest success. Physicians could, however, raise or affirm suspicions that the afflictions had supernatural causes. An example of this would be Cotton Mather's description of the diagnosis of the Goodwin children. He wrote, "Skillful Physicians were consulted for their Help, and particularly our worthy and prudent Friend Dr. Thomas Oakes, who found himself so affronted by the Distempers of the children, that he concluded nothing but a hellish Witchcraft could be the Original of these Maladies."[352]

Concerning the Warboys case, two physicians from Cambridge diagnosed Jane Throckmorton as being bewitched. Several members of the Royal College of Physicians had examined Mary Glover before her trial. Highly respected Oxford physicians had attempted to cure Anne Gunter. Samuel Pacy asked Dr. Feavor for a diagnosis of his daughter, just as John Goodwin prevailed upon Dr. Oakes and others for their expertise. At Salem, Reverend Parris consulted several physicians concerning the illnesses of Betty Parris and Abigail Williams before seeking the guidance of other ministers. The opinions of these doctors carried great weight, especially in regards to the unfolding of the events at Salem. A less supernatural diagnosis from the physicians could have possibly led to the witch trials not taking place.

Clergymen also visited the sufferers as well in hopes of healing the afflictions. When William Somers fell ill with symptoms similar to epilepsy, Reverend John Darrell diagnosed witchcraft and promised a cure through dispossession. At Warboys, the children's uncle, Reverend Dorington, regularly visited the children and prayed for them. Leading doctors of divinity from Oxford, including two future bishops, attended to Anne Gunter.[353] Several unnamed Puritan ministers prayed with the Glover family, eventually curing Mary during a large public dispossession shortly after the trial of Elizabeth Jackson. Though Samuel Pacy did not mention the participation of clergymen in his deposition, which does not mean it did not occur. The well-respected and influential Reverends Allen, Moody, Willard, and Cotton Mather prayed and fasted at the Goodwin household. At Salem, after the physicians could not cure the girls, Reverend Parris asked the advice of several ministers, who prayed and fasted at the Parris parsonage, but with no success.

Friends and family of the afflicted endeavored to cure the afflicted through popular remedies including counter-witchcraft. Allies of the Gunters burned the thatch of Elizabeth Gregory's house and Lady Cromwell cut off some of Agnes Samuel's hair, two procedures considered effective at diminishing a witch's power. At the Bury St. Edmunds trial, Dorothy Durrant deposed that Amy Denny suffered burns when her familiar, a toad, was thrown into a fire. These folk remedies occurred alongside of religious techniques such as public dispossession, which occurred in the cases involving John Darrell and Mary Glover. In short, there was a wide variety of methods available to attempt to cure the afflicted.

Our seven cases also show that the accused witches showed a number of broad similarities in terms of poor socio-economic standing and community relations. In many ways, the characteristics of the accused witches in our case studies are similar to those discussed in Alan Macfarlane's study of accused witches in his *Witchcraft in Tudor and Stuart England: A Regional and Comparative Study*, though he did not include possession cases.[354] Macfarlane found the community regarded suspected witches as contentious, troublesome, malevolent, and argumentative,[355] which is certainly true in our cases. Elizabeth Gregory was said to be "...a notorious scolding body & a vile curser & blasphemer,"[356] Sarah Good had "...so turbulent a spirit, spiteful, and so maliciously bent,"[357] and Alice Samuel had a "naughty manner of living," combined with "negligent coming to church and slackness in God's service."[358] According to Cotton Mather, the widow Glover was "an ignorant and a scandalous old Woman" and a "Hag."[359] Some, such as Agnes Pepwell in the Anne Gunter case, Amy Denny and Rose Cullender at the Bury St. Edmunds trial, the widow Glover of Boston, and Bridget Bishop at Salem, already had reputations for witchcraft by the time they were accused.[360]

This unpopularity in the community is particularly noticeable at the trials of the accused witches. The bewitchment of the afflicted tended to be the catalyst for the trial and the most important charge against the accused, but it was rarely the only one. At the trials of the Samuels, Elizabeth Jackson, Elizabeth Gregory and the Pepwells, Amy Denny and Rose Cullender, the widow Glover, and, most notably, at Salem, members of the community testified about previous witchlike activities of the accused, activities that may have occurred many years before. The collective memory of the community helped create and solidify the reputation of a witch.

Another characteristic of witchcraft accusations described in *Witchcraft in Tudor and Stuart England: A Regional and Comparative Study* and our case studies is the proximity between the accusers and the accused witches' homes. Macfarlane's research discovered the accusers lived close to the accused, sometimes as next-door neighbors.[361] It appears it was tensions between neighbors, unsolvable by other means, which led to the accusations. This is true in all of our cases excepting

Salem, where the accusers occasionally accused people they had never even seen.

Macfarlane described suspected witches as middle-aged or elderly, with their victims typically a generation younger.[362] With few exceptions, this applies to our case studies as well, though it is difficult to prove as the surviving documents rarely give exact ages. Macfarlane also found that the community rarely suspected unmarried women of witchcraft, though wives and widows were.[363] Again, this roughly correlates to our examples, as Alice Samuel, Elizabeth Gregory, Sarah Good, Sarah Osborne, Martha Corey, and Rebecca Nurse were all married at the time of their trials, and Elizabeth Jackson, the widow Glover, Amy Denny, and Rose Cullender were widows. Most of these women had children, which, as Macfarlane explains, was no guarantee against accusations of witchcraft.[364]

Of course, there were exceptions to these patterns. At Salem, accusations were made against some of the most powerful, well-respected, and wealthy members of the community. As the trials continued, accusations came from people of all ages and occupations, who sometimes had never even seen those they had accused. Occasionally, the authorities executed men as well as women, specifically John Samuel at Warboys and John Proctor, Reverend George Burroughs, George Jacobs, John Willard, and Samuel Wardwell at Salem. John Darrell tutored both young men and women to feign possession. In addition, popularity aside, not all of the accused were without influential advocates. Elizabeth Jackson received support from the testimony of Doctors Jorden and Argent during the Mary Glover case, while the testimony of Brian Gunter's relative, Thomas Hinton, led to the freeing of Elizabeth Gregory and the Pepwells. At Salem, friends and family of the accused presented several petitions to the Court of Oyer and Terminer, attesting to the respectability and blameless lives of several of the defendants.

Our seven case studies reveal that the families of the possessed girls were generally wealthier than the accused witches. Robert Throckmorton, Brian Gunter, Samuel Pacy, and Thomas Putnam were among the richest men in their villages, if not the richest. The afflicted children tended to come from church going, respected, relatively wealthy, well-connected, literate families that had little difficulty in mobilizing allies in the community against the accused. Though as young females the afflicted assumed restricted and submissive roles within their family, they belonged to a higher social class than the accused witches did. Salem again proved the exception, as the pious and well-respected Rebecca Nurse was hanged and the wealthy Carys and Englishes were forced to flee.

Our case studies point to another generalization, namely that the afflicted children usually experienced strict religious upbringing. The Throckmorton children read their Bibles and said family prayers twice a day, while their uncle, Reverend Dorington, was a frequent visitor.[365] Mary Glover was raised in a strict Puritan household and her grandfather was burned at the stake for his religious beliefs.[366] According to Cotton Mather, John Goodwin had "…a Religious Family" and his children "…enjoyed a Religious Education, and answered it with a very towardly Ingenuity."[367] The Salem witchcraft trials began with the afflictions suffered by Betty Parris and Abigail Williams at Reverend Samuel Parris' parsonage. Here, the pressures and strains upon Reverend Parris, along with his sermons and prayers concerning witchcraft and Satan could easily have affected these two young, impressionable girls.

This leads to the interesting generalization that in almost every case the possessed reacted strongly against prayers and readings from the Bible. For example, describing the Goodwin children, Cotton Mather wrote:

> Much more, All Praying to God, and Reading of his Word, would occasion a very terrible Vexation to them: they would then stop their own Ears with their own Hands; and roar, and shriek; and holla, to drown the Voice of the Devotion. Yea, if anyone in the Room took up a Bible to look into it, tho the Children could see nothing of it, as being in a crowd of Spectators, or having their

Faces another way, yet would they be in wonderful Miseries, till the Bible were laid aside.[368]

In *Mary Glovers Late Woeful Case*, Steven Bradwell used this revulsion against the word of God to demonstrate how Mary was not suffering from a natural disease:

> In so much, as when one of the preachers, in the middest of those blasphemous abusions of Godds goodly image, prayed God to rebuke that foule malicious divell, she suddenly (saith the storie) though blinde, dumbe and deafe, turned to him, and did bark out froath at him. So did she to others that stood over her, cast out foam, up to their faces; her mouth being wide open. There is no cause, that I can understand, whie the suffocation of the mother should have been in such a chafe.[369]

Once these cases reached the trial stage, in every instance judges exercised great influence over the final verdict. As we have seen, Judges Fenner, Anderson, Hale, Hathorne, and Stoughton were able to coerce witnesses, the accused witches, and/or the juries. At the Warboys trial, Judge Fenner threatened John Samuel with execution unless Samuel swore an oath in which he confessed to witchcraft, which directly led to Samuel's subsequent hanging. In the Mary Glover case, Judge Anderson firmly intended to influence the jury when he stated that Elizabeth Jackson fit the description of a witch. Judges Hathorne and Corwin clearly encouraged the accusers, as well as the accused, to name additional witches, a practice unique in our case studies to Salem. At Rebecca Nurse's trial at Salem, Judge Stoughton rejected the jury's decision of not guilty, making them deliberate again until they returned a guilty verdict.

Though to modern sensibilities it looks as if misguided judges willfully executed people for crimes they could not possibly have committed, in reality judges were responsible for enforcing a perfectly reasonable law for the time. People took witchcraft seriously as a crime deserving capital punishment. In our case studies, if the judges believed the evidence warranted an execution, they could influence the jury towards one. Yet, the opinions of the judges were not monolithic. At the conclusion of the Abingdon trial of Elizabeth Gregory and the Pepwells in 1605, Justices Christopher Yelverton and David Williams, who had helped write the Witchcraft Act of 1604, found the women not guilty of witchcraft against Anne Gunter.

Though the symptoms of the afflicted and the reactions of their families were similar in many respects, we have noticed that vastly different interpretations and conclusions sprung from possession cases. Possession cases frequently became catalysts for displaying larger and more important issues than a youthful individual's health, issues in which the participants manipulated the possession for a variety of reasons, including personal aggrandizement, social animosity, religious rivalry, and political machinations. People like John Darrell and Brian Gunter crafted possession cases for reasons entirely separate from the well-being of the adolescents in their care. Physicians (occasionally disagreeing at the same trial) employed contemporary medical theories to "verify" both the natural and supernatural causes of possession. Possession cases acted as a prism whereby interpretations ran a full spectrum from honest concern to outright fraud.

Ecclesiastical and civil leadership usually played an important role in keeping the passions and accusations of the people in check. In each of our cases, except Salem, though a disreputable witch or two, unpopular in the community, were accused, prosecuted, and possibly executed, possession cases rarely led to a bona fide witch-hunt. An execution seemed to alleviate local fears and tensions, especially if the afflicted found relief from the supernatural symptoms.

As in several of the generalizations, Salem proved to be a dramatic exception to this rule. Here the judicial leadership did not dampen or limit the anxiety and accusations, but allowed them to spread to several surrounding towns. The members of the Court of Oyer and Terminer literally found everyone accused guilty. The accusations did not stop with stereotypical witches, as in other cases. Some of the most powerful and wealthy people in Massachusetts were accused of sending their specters to torment the girls, even though they had never seen the accused before. In a complete reversal from other witchcraft trials, the judges had only the people who refused to confess executed. Much of the evidence presented that led to their deaths was spectral evidence and the testimony of young girls and confessed witches. This was supplemented by testimony consisting of malicious rumors, gossip, and hearsay between neighbors, over events that could have occurred decades before. As the jails filled and hangings took place, the afflictions of the girls did not end, which was unusual in cases of possession. Arrests and accusations continued, as witch hysteria overwhelmed Salem and its neighboring towns.

Though we can reach some tentative generalizations about demonic possession in these cases, there are still intriguing unresolved issues. Although Anne Gunter swore her father forced her to counterfeit the possession, why did several members of Oxford's elite testify to her bewitchment, even to her ability to grow heavier and a foot taller during her fits?[370] Why did the authorities at Salem sustain the accusations without critical evaluation and allow them to spread so far? Was fourteen-year-old Mary Glover a pawn, another vehicle for propaganda, for Puritan enthusiasts? Did children's imagination and play-acting turn malicious and finally murderous in any of our examples? How many accusers and magistrates really pursued their own agendas, which had little to do with witchcraft or illness?

Other than Ann Putnam, Jr. of Salem Village, the youthful accusers themselves left no answers. We do not know if any of them felt remorse or satisfaction over their involvement in the deaths of innocent people. Apart from their names occasionally appearing in parish registers at the time of their marriage and death, they disappear from the record books.

Ann Putnam Jr., however, presents an interesting and heartfelt dénouement for her participation in the Salem trials. Unfortunately, none of the other accusers in our case studies left such a confession. In

1706, she stood in front of the congregation at the Salem Village church, while Reverend Green (Reverend Parris' replacement) read her words:

> ...that I, then being in my childhood, should, by such a providence of God, be made an instrument for the accusing of several persons of a grievous crime, whereby their lives were taken away from them, whom now I have just grounds and good reason to believe they were innocent persons; and that it was a great delusion of Satan that deceived me in that sad time, whereby I justly fear I have been instrumental, with others, though ignorantly and unwittingly, to bring upon myself and this land the guilt of innocent blood; though what was said or done by me against any person I can truly and uprightly say, before God and man, I did it not out of any anger, malice, or ill-will to any person, for I had no such thing against one of them; but what I did was ignorantly, being deluded by Satan. And particularly, as I was a chief instrument of accusing of Goodwife Nurse and her two sisters, I desire to lie in the dust, and to be humbled for it, in that I was a cause, with others, of so sad a calamity to them and their families; for which cause I desire to lie in the dust, and earnestly beg forgiveness of God, and from all those unto whom I have given just cause of sorrow and offence, whose relations were taken away or accused.[371]

Unfortunately, the thinness of the historical record leads us to few unambiguous conclusions. While they lived in far different times than we do, with a ubiquitous belief in the supernatural, we also see their suspicion and sympathy, fear and faith, greed and godliness, and compassion and cruelty. The examination of possession trials provides us with a deeper understanding and awareness of the culture in which they took place by reaffirming that the participants of these trials shared many of the same inherent human characteristics still around today.

Endnotes

INTRODUCTION: POSSESSION IN HISTORY

[1] Reverend John Hale, "A Modest Enquiry into the Nature of Witchcraft," in *Narratives of the Witchcraft Cases, 1648-1706*, ed. George Lincoln Burr (New York: C. Scribner's Sons, 1914), 413.

[2] George Lyman Kittredge, *Witchcraft in Old and New England* (Cambridge, MA: Harvard University Press, 1929), 304-305.

[3] Simon Kemp and Kevin Williams, "Demonic Possession and Mental Disorders in Medieval and Early Modern Europe," *Psychological Medicine* 17 (1987): 22.

[4] Ilza Veith, *Hysteria: The History of a Disease* (Chicago: University of Chicago Press, 1965), 40-2.

[5] Brian Levack, *Possession and Exorcism* (New York: Garland Publishing, 1992), ix.

[6] Brian Levack, "Possession, Witchcraft, and the Law in Jacobean England," *Washington and Lee Law Review* 52 (1996): 1621.

[7] D.P. Walker, *Unclean Spirits: Possession and Exorcism in France and England in the Late Sixteenth and Early Seventeenth Centuries* (Philadelphia: University of Pennsylvania Press, 1981), 8-9. For more detailed information on demonic possession in the Bible, see Stevan L. Davies, *Jesus The Healer: Possession, Trance, and the Origins of Christianity* (New York: The Continuum Publishing Company, 1995).

[8] Moshe Sluhovsky, "A Divine Apparition or Demonic Possession? Female Agency and Church Authority in Sixteenth-Century France," *Sixteenth Century Journal* 27 (1996): 1043-44.

[9] Levack, "Possession, Witchcraft, and the Law in Jacobean England," 1614.

[10] Barbara Rosen, *Witchcraft in England: 1558-1618* (Amherst, MA: University of Massachusetts Press, 1991), 32-33.

[11] Nancy Caciola, "Mystics, Demoniacs, and the Physiology of Spirit Possession in Medieval Europe," *Comparative Studies in Society and History*, 42 (April 2000): 268-9, 272, 295. See also Barbara Newman, "Possessed by the Spirit: Devout Women, Demoniacs, and the Apostolic Life in the Thirteenth Century," *Speculum* 73 (1998): 733-770.

[12] Caciola, 269.

[13] Caciola, 279.

[14] Keith Thomas, *Religion and the Decline of Magic* (New York: Charles Scribner's Sons, 1971), 482-86.

[15] Nicholas P. Spanos, *Multiple Identities and False Memories* (Washington, D.C.: American Psychological Association, 1996), 162.

[16] Sandar L. Gilman, Helen King, Roy Porter, G.S. Rousseau, Elaine Showalter, *Hysteria Beyond Freud*, Berkeley, CA.: University of California Press, 1993), 98-99.

[17] William Monter, *Ritual, Myth and Magic in Early Modern Europe* (Athens, Ohio: Ohio University Press, 1984), 87-8.

[18] Jonathan L. Pearl, "'A School for the Rebel Soul': Politics and Demonic Possession in France," *Historical Reflections* 16 (1989): 290-92.

[19] An interesting example occurred in Marseilles in 1610-11, when two Ursuline novices accused their confessor of rape and witchcraft. Recounted in Michelle Marshman, "Exorcism as Empowerment: A New Idiom," *The Journal of Religious History* 23 (October 1999): 265-281.

[20] Brian Levack, *The Witch-hunt in Early Modern Europe* (New York: Garland Publishing, 1987), 155.

[21] Robin Briggs, *Witches & Neighbors: The Social and Cultural Context of European Witchcraft* (New York: Viking, 1996), 214-5. For full accounts of the Loudun trials, see Michel de Certeau, *The Possession at Loudun* (Chicago: The University of Chicago Press, 2000); and Robert Rapley, *A Case of Witchcraft: The Trial of Urbain Grandier* (Montreal: McGill-Queen's University Press, 1998).

[22] Briggs, 215.

Two Families In Conflict: The Possessions at Warboys

[23] D.P. Walker, *Unclean Spirits: Possession and Exorcism in France and England in the Late Sixteenth and Early Seventeenth Centuries* (Philadelphia: University of Pennsylvania Press, 1981), 50.

[24] Moira Tatem, *The Witches of Warboys* (Cambridgeshire, U.K.: Cambridgeshire Libraries Publications, 1993), 9. For an in-depth examination of witchcraft pamphlets, including the Warboys pamphlet, see Marion Gibson, *Reading Witchcraft: Stories of Early English Witches* (London: Routledge, 1999).

[25] Anne Reiber DeWindt, "Witchcraft and Conflicting Visions of the Ideal Village Community," *Journal of British Studies* 34 (October 1995): 439; Tatem, 10,11,16.

[26] *The Most Strange and Admirable Discoverie of the Three Witches of Warboys* (London: Widdowe Orwin, 1593), *in Witchcraft in England, 1558-1618,* ed. Barbara Rosen (Amherst, MA: The University of Massachusetts Press, 1969, 1991), 229, 240f.

[27] DeWindt, 436.

[28] DeWindt, 436-7; Tatem, 15.

[29] Tatem, 17, 74.

[30] DeWindt, 438.

[31] Tatem, 16-17.

[32] Tatem, 19-21.

[33] *Most Strange and Admirable Discoverie,* in Rosen, 241.

[34] *Most Strange and Admirable Discoverie,* in Rosen, 242.

[35] *Most Strange and Admirable Discoverie,* in Rosen, 242-3; Tatem, 17.

[36] *Most Strange and Admirable Discoverie,* in Rosen, 243-4.

[37] *Most Strange and Admirable Discoverie,* in Rosen, 247.

[38] *Most Strange and Admirable Discoverie,* in Rosen, 246-7.

[39] Tatem, 35.

[40] *Most Strange and Admirable Discoverie,* in Rosen; 252; Tatem, 34.

[41] Tatem, 33.

[42] *Most Strange and Admirable Discoverie,* in Rosen, 253f.

[43] *Most Strange and Admirable Discoverie,* in Rosen, 254.

[44] Walker, 51.

[45] Tatem, 39.

[46] Tatem, 39.

[47] Michael MacDonald, *Witchcraft and Hysteria in Elizabethan London: Edward Jorden and the Mary Glover Case* (London: Tavistock/Routledge, 1991), xi; see also Stuart Clark, *Thinking With Demons: The Idea of Witchcraft in Early Modern Europe* (Oxford: Oxford University Press, 1997), 280-282.

[48] Keith Thomas, *Religion and the Decline of Magic* (New York: Charles Scribner's Sons, 1971), 523-4.

[49] Tatem, 43.

[50] *Most Strange and Admirable Discoverie,* in Rosen, 261.

[51] Tatem, 44.

[52] Tatem, 45.

[53] Tatem, 45.

[54] *Most Strange and Admirable Discoverie,* in Rosen, 263.

[55] Walker, 50-51.

[56] *Most Strange and Admirable Discoverie,* in Rosen, 249.

[57] *Most Strange and Admirable Discoverie,* in Rosen, 282-3; Tatem, 16.

[58] *Most Strange and Admirable Discoverie,* in Rosen, 283.

[59] *Most Strange and Admirable Discoverie,* in Rosen, 265.

[60] Tatem, 53.

[61] Tatem, 53.

[62] Tatem, 62.

[63] *Most Strange and Admirable Discoverie,* in Rosen, 290.

[64] *Most Strange and Admirable Discoverie,* in Rosen, 291.

[65] George Lyman Kittredge, *Witchcraft in Old and New England* (Cambridge, MA: Harvard University Press, 1929), 304-305.

[66] Kittredge, 306-313.

POSSESSION, PURITANISM, AND POLITICS: THE CASES OF JOHN DARRELL & MARY GLOVER

[67] Michael MacDonald, *Witchcraft and Hysteria in Elizabethan London: Edward Jorden and the Mary Glover Case* (London: Tavistock/Routledge, 1991), x.

[68] Arthur F. Kinney and David W. Swain, eds., *Tudor England: An Encyclopedia* (New York: Garland Publishing, 2001), 21, 575-7.

[69] Stephen Greenblatt, "Exorcism Into Art," *Representations* 12 (Autumn, 1985): 16; MacDonald, xix-xx.

[70] D.P. Walker, *Unclean Spirits: Possession and Exorcism in France and England in the Late Sixteenth and Early Seventeenth Centuries* (Philadelphia: University of Pennsylvania Press, 1981), 10.

[71] Greenblatt, 16; James Sharpe, *Instruments of Darkness: Witchcraft in Early Modern England* (Philadelphia: University of Pennsylvania Press, 1996), 194-5.

[72] Richard Raiswell, "'Faking It': A Case of Counterfeit Possession in the Reign of James I," *Renaissance and Reformation* 23 (Summer 1999): 39.

[73] F.W. Brownlow, *Shakespeare, Harsnett, and the Devils of Denham* (Newark: University of Delaware Press), 62.

[74] Walker, 73.

[75] Brownlow, 52-53; Keith Thomas, *Religion and the Decline of Magic* (New York: Charles Scribner's Sons, 1971), 483-6.

[76] Corinne Holt Rickert, *The Case of John Darrell: Minister and Exorcist* (Gainesville: University of Florida, 1962), 12-13.

[77] Sir Leslie Stephen and Sir Sidney Lee, eds., *The Dictionary of National Biography* (London: Oxford University Press, 1917), 374-5; Kinney and Swain, 92-93.

[78] Brownlow, 54f. According to Marion Gibson, the pamphlet was written by Jesse Bee, John Denison, and possibly others. See Marion Gibson, *Reading Witchcraft: Stories of Early English Witches* (London: Routledge, 1999), 40.

[79] MacDonald, xxi.

[80] Brownlow, 55; Walker, 59.

[81] Brownlow, 56; Walker, 62.

[82] Walker, 62.

[83] Walker, 62.

[84] Brownlow, 56; Walker, 64.

[85] MacDonald, xxi.

[86] Walker, 63.

[87] MacDonald, xxii.

[88] MacDonald, xxii; Walker, 64.

[89] Walker, 62.

[90] Rickert, 55.

[91] For a general discussion on James' views concerning religion during his reign, see James Doelman, *King James I and the Religious Culture of England* (Cambridge: D.S. Brewster, 2000) and Kenneth Fincham and Peter Lake, "The Ecclesiastical Policy of King James I," *Journal of British Studies* 24 (April 1985): 169-207.

[92] MacDonald, xxv-xxvi.

[93] For a discussion of Jorden's views on "suffocation of the mother," see G.S. Rousseau, "'A Strange Pathology' History in the Modern World, 1500-1800," in Sandar L. Gilman, Helen King, Roy Porter, G.S. Rousseau, Elaine Showalter, *Hysteria Beyond Freud* (Berkeley, CA: University of California Press, 1993), 116-124. On "suffocation of the mother" throughout history, see Harold Merskey and Susan J. Merskey, "Hysteria, or 'suffocation of the mother,'" *History of Medicine* 148 (February 1993): 399-405.

[94] MacDonald, xii; Sharpe, 191.

[95] Stephen Bradwell, *Mary Glovers Late Woeful Case* (London: n.p., 1603), in MacDonald, 3.

[96] MacDonald, xiii.

[97] MacDonald, xii.

[98] MacDonald, xi.

[99] Bradwell in MacDonald, 4.

[100] MacDonald, xli.

[101] MacDonald, xiii.

[102] MacDonald, xlv.

[103] MacDonald, xiii-xiv.

[104] MacDonald, xlvi.

[105] MacDonald, xlvi.

[106] Bradwell in MacDonald, 23-24.

[107] MacDonald, xiv-xv.

[108] Carroll Camden, "The Suffocation of the Mother," *Modern Language Notes* 63 (June, 1948): 391-2.

[109] Bradwell in MacDonald, 29.

[110] Bradwell in MacDonald, 28-9.

[111] MacDonald, xviii.

[112] MacDonald, xviii-xix.

[113] MacDonald, xix.

[114] John Swan, *A True and Briefe Report of Mary Glovers Vexation* (n.p., 1603) in MacDonald, 46-7.

[115] MacDonald, xxv.

[116] Swan in MacDonald, 46-47.

[117] Jorden in MacDonald; MacDonald, viii. xxiii, xxiv.

[118] MacDonald, xxv.

[119] Raiswell, 39; Walker, 77.

[120] Brownlow, 64.

[121] Sharpe, 153.

THE ANNE GUNTER CASE: AN ILL GIRL, A PERFIDIOUS FATHER, AND A SKEPTICAL KING

[122] James Sharpe, *The Bewitching of Anne Gunter: A Horrible and True Story of Deception, Witchcraft, Murder and the King of England* (New York: Routledge, 2000), 116.

[123] Sharpe, 116.

[124] Christine Larner, *Witchcraft and Religion: The Politics of Popular Belief* (New York: Basil Blackwell, 1984), 13-15. Deborah Willis, *Malevolent Nurture: Witch-Hunting and Maternal Power in Early Modern England* (Ithaca: Cornell University Press, 1995), 124-158. For more information on James views towards witchcraft, see Stuart Clark, "King James's Daemonologie: Witchcraft and Kingship," in *The Damned Art: Essays in the Literature of Witchcraft*, ed. Sydney Anglo (London: Routledge and Kegan Paul, 1977), 156-181; and Lawrence Normand and Gareth Roberts, *Witchcraft in Early Modern Scotland: James VI's Demonology and the North Berwick Witches* (Exeter: University of Exeter Press, 2000), which includes the full text of James' *Daemonologie*.

[125] Larner, 9-10.

[126] Larner, 9-15.

[127] Ronald Holmes, *Witchcraft in British History* (London: Frederick Muller Limited, 1974), 136-7. The swim test occurred when accused witches were bound and tossed into a body of water, the theory being the water would "reject" the impure witch. If the accused witch sank, she could be considered innocent, provided she survived.

[128] Larner, 5.

[129] Rosemary Ellen Guiley, *The Encyclopedia of Witches and Witchcraft*, 2nd ed. (New York: Checkmark Books, 1999), 178-9; Sharpe, 117.

[130] Larner, 18-20.

[131] Guiley, 178.

[132] Guiley, 178.

[133] D.P. Walker, *Unclean Spirits: Possession and Exorcism in France and England in the Late Sixteenth and Early Seventeenth Centuries* (Philadelphia: University of Pennsylvania Press, 1981), 77.

[134] Sharpe, xi., 211.

[135] Sharpe, 14, 22-3, 37-9.

[136] Sharpe, 14-19.

[137] Sharpe, 43.

[138] Sharpe, 30-1.

[139] Sharpe, 44.

[140] Sharpe, 45.

[141] Sharpe, 46-7.

[142] Sharpe, xi., 48-50.

[143] Sharpe, 49.

[144] Sharpe, 33, 40-1.

[145] Sharpe, 48.

[146] Sharpe, 48, 170-1.

[147] Sharpe, 54.

[148] Sharpe, 53-4.

[149] Sharpe, 6-10.

[150] Sharpe, 60-62.

[151] Sharpe, 52.

[152] Sharpe, 92.

[153] Sharpe, 99-100.

[154] Sharpe, 100-2.

[155] Sharpe, 108.

[156] Sharpe, 114.

[157] Sharpe, 128.

[158] Sharpe, 128-9.

[159] Sharpe, 137.

[160] Sharpe, 102-4, 106-7.

[161] Sharpe, 103.

[162] Brian Levack, "Possession, Witchcraft, and the Law in Jacobean England," *Washington and Lee Law Review* 52 (1996): 1623.

[163] Sharpe, 134-7.

[164] Sharpe, 134.

[165] Sharpe, 135.

[166] Sharpe, 131.

[167] Sharpe, 131.

[168] Levack, 1625-6.

[169] Sharpe, 178-9.

[170] Sharpe, 182.

[171] Sharpe, 184.

[172] Sharpe, 180, 184, 186-7.

[173] Sharpe, 179.

[174] Sharpe, 180.

[175] Sharpe, 163.

[176] Sharpe, 10-12.

[177] Sharpe, 1-2.

[178] Sharpe, 192.

[179] Sharpe, 192.

[180] Sharpe, 135, 163-5.

[181] Sharpe, 194-5.

[182] Levack, 1636.

EXECUTIONS, EVIDENCE & THE INTELLECTUAL ELITES: THE TRIAL AT BURY ST. EDMUNDS

[183] Gilbert Geis and Ivan Bunn, *A Trial of Witches: A Seventeenth-Century Witchcraft Prosecution* (London: Routledge, 1997), 7; Rosemary Ellen Guiley *The Encyclopedia of Witches and Witchcraft* 2nd edition (New York: Checkmark Books, 1999), 40; Rossell Hope Robbins, *The Encyclopedia of Witchcraft and Demonology* (New York: Crown Publishers, Inc., 1959), 66.

[184] Geis and Bunn, 9, 10, 26, 27.

[185] Geis and Bunn, 14-20.

[186] Unknown author, as quoted in Geis and Bunn, 216

[187] Geis and Bunn, 61.

[188] Geis and Bunn, 217.

[189] Unknown author, as quoted in Geis and Bunn, 217.

[190] Unknown author, as quoted in Geis and Bunn, 218.

[191] Unknown author, as quoted in Geis and Bunn, 218.

[192] Guiley, 7.

[193] Unknown author, as quoted in Geis and Bunn, 219.

[194] Geis and Bunn, 219.

[195] Unknown author, as quoted in Geis and Bunn, 220.

[196] Geis and Bunn, 70-72.

[197] Unknown author, as quoted in Geis and Bunn, 213.

[198] Geis and Bunn, 213-14.

[199] Unknown author, as quoted in Geis and Bunn, 215.

[200] Geis and Bunn, 214-15.

[201] Geis and Bunn, 215-6.

[202] Geis and Bunn, 221-2.

[203] Geis and Bunn, 70-1.

[204] Unknown author, as quoted in Geis and Bunn, 220.

[205] Unknown author, as quoted in Geis and Bunn, 82-3.

[206] Unknown author, as quoted in Geis and Bunn, 223-4.

[207] Geis and Bunn, 135.

[208] Unknown author, as quoted in Geis and Bunn, 224.

[209] Unknown author, as quoted in Geis and Bunn, 224.

[210] Unknown author, as quoted in Geis and Bunn, 224-5.

[211] Geis and Bunn, 34-5.

[212] Unknown author, as quoted in Geis and Bunn, 226.

[213] Geis and Bunn, 225-6.

[214] Unknown author, as quoted in Geis and Bunn, 227.

[215] Unknown author, as quoted in Geis and Bunn, 227.

[216] Unknown author, as quoted in Geis and Bunn, 227.

[217] Unknown author, as quoted in Geis and Bunn, 228.

[218] William Parmly Dunn, *Sir Thomas Browne: A Study in Religious Philosophy* (MN: University of Minnesota Press, 1950), 43-4.

[219] Sir Thomas Browne, *This Special Edition of Religio Medici* (Birmingham, AL: The Classics of Medicine Library, 1981), 78-9.

[220] Alan Cromartie, *Sir Mathew Hale: 1609-1676* (Cambridge: Cambridge University Press, 1995), 6.

[221] Geis and Bunn, 82.

[222] Geis and Bunn, 165.

[223] Geis and Bunn, 17.

[224] Keith Thomas, *Religion and the Decline of Magic* (New York: Charles Scribner's Sons, 1971), 570-83.

[225] Edmund Gosse, *Sir Thomas Browne* (London: Macmillan and Co., Limited, 1924), 147.

[226] Edmund Heward, *Matthew Hale* (London: Robert Hale & Company, 1972), 86.

[227] Geis and Bunn, 7-8.

[228] Cotton Mather, *Wonders of the Invisible World* (London: John Russell Smith, 1693,1862), 111.

[229] Mather, 111.

[230] Carol F. Karlsen, *The Devil in the Shape of a Woman: Witchcraft in Colonial New England* (New York: W.W. Norton & Company, 1998) 233.

[231] James Sharpe, *Instruments of Darkness: Witchcraft in Early Modern England* (Philadelphia: University of Pennsylvania Press, 1996), 226.

THE FORESHADOWING OF SALEM: THE GOODWIN CHILDREN & A HANGING IN BOSTON

[232] David D. Hall, ed. *Witch-Hunting in Seventeenth-Century New England* (Boston: Northeastern University Press, 1991), 11.

[233] Frederick C. Drake, "Witchcraft in the American Colonies, 1647-62," *American Quarterly* 20 (Winter, 1968): 711.

[234] Sanford J. Fox, *Science and Justice: The Massachusetts Witchcraft Trials* (Baltimore: The Johns Hopkins Press, 1968), 36-7. Richard Godbeer, *The Devil's Dominion: Magic and Religion in Early New England.* (Cambridge: Cambridge University Press, 1992), 153.

[235] Hall, Appendix, 315-6.

[236] Hall, 4

[237] John Demos, *Entertaining Satan* (New York: Oxford University Press, 1982), 341.

[238] Hall, 11.

[239] Richard Godbeer, *The Devil's Dominion* (Cambridge: Cambridge University Press, 1992), 41-2; Carol F. Karlsen, *The Devil in the Shape of a Woman: Witchcraft in Colonial New England.* New York: W.W. Norton & Company, 1998. 7.

[240] Thomas, 523-4

[241] Cotton Mather in Burr, 100-101.

[242] Cotton Mather in Burr, 99.

[243] Cotton Mather in Hall, 268.

[244] Mather in Burr, 101-2.

[245] Cotton Mather, *Memorable Providences, Relating to Witchcrafts and Possessions* in Hall, 267-8.

[246] Chadwick Hansen, *Witchcraft at Salem* (New York, George Braziller, 1969), 21; Cotton Mather in Hall, 269-276.

[247] Mather in Hall, 268-270.

[248] Mather in Hall, 270.

[249] Mather in Burr, 103.

[250] Mather in Burr, 104.

[251] Mather in Burr, 104.

[252] Mather in Burr, 105.

[253] Mather in Burr, 107-8.

[254] David Harley, "Explaining Salem: Calvinist Psychology and the Diagnosis of Possession," *The American Historical Review* 101 (April 1996): 314.

[255] Mather in Burr, 110-1.

[256] Mather in Burr, 112.

[257] Willard in Burr, 112-3.

[258] Mather in Burr, 112-3.

[259] Mather in Bur, 117.

[260] Mather in Burr, 118.

[261] Mather in Burr, 120.

[262] Mather in Burr, 120-1.

[263] Mather in Burr, 124-6.

[264] Hansen, 27-8.; Karlsen, 34-5.

[265] Kenneth Silverman, *The Life and Times of Cotton Mather* (New York: Harper & Row, 1984), 87.

[266] Silverman, 43.

[267] Winslow, 117.

[268] Frances Hill, *A Delusion of Satan: The Full Story of the Salem Witch Trials* (New York: Doubleday, 1995), 20.

[269] Hansen, 22-3.

[270] Godbeer, 112-116; Mather in Burr, 137-140.

SALEM: THE SELF-DESTRUCTION OF A NEW ENGLAND COMMUNITY BY POSSESSION AND PANIC

[271] Carol F. Karlsen, *The Devil in the Shape of A Woman: Witchcraft in Colonial New England* (New York: W.W. Norton & Company, 1998), 24-51, 240.

[272] Linnda R. Caporael, "Ergotism: The Satan Loosed in Salem," *Science* 192 (April 2, 1976): 21-6; Laurie Winn Carlson, *A Fever in Salem* (Chicago: Ivan R. Dee, 1999), 117-8, 123-4, Karlsen, 233, 250-51; Frances Hill, *A Delusion of Satan: The Full Story of the Salem Witch Tri-

als (New York: Doubleday, 1995), 20; Alan Woolf, "Witchcraft or Mycotoxin? The Salem Witch Trials," *Journal of Toxicology. Clinical Toxicology* 38 (2000): 457-60.

[273] Paul Boyer and Stephen Nissenbaum, *Salem Possessed: The Social Origins of Witchcraft* (Cambridge, MA: Harvard University Press, 1974), 80-132.

[274] Chadwick Hansen, *Witchcraft at Salem* (New York: Braziller, 1969), 64-73.

[275] For information concerning Dr. Griggs and the original diagnosis of the children, see Norman Gevitz "'The Devil Hath Laughed at the Physicians': Witchcraft and Medical Practices in Seventeenth-Century New England," *Journal of the History of Medicine and Allied Sciences* 55 (January 2000): 30-1. For information concerning the complex relationship between religion and medicine in Puritan New England, see Patricia A. Watson, *The Angelical Conjunction: The Preacher-Physicians of Colonial New England*. (Knoxville, TN: The University of Tennessee Press, 1991).

[276] Hansen, 31.

[277] Peter Charles Hoffer, *The Devil's Disciples: Makers of the Salem Witchcraft Trials* (Baltimore: The Johns Hopkins University Press, 1996), 106-9.

[278] The subject of the legal aspects of the Salem trials has attracted a number of interesting works. See Sanford J. Fox, *Science and Justice: The Massachusetts Witchcraft Trials* (Baltimore: The Johns Hopkins Press, 1968); Peter Charles Hoffer, *The Salem Witchcraft Trials: A Legal History* (Lawrence, Kansas: University Press of Kansas, 1997); Bernard Rosenthal, *Salem Story: Reading the Witch Trials of 1692* (Cambridge: Cambridge University Press, 1993); David Thomas Konig, *Law and Society in Puritan Massachusetts: Essex County, 1629-*

1692 (Chapel Hill: The University of North Carolina Press, 1979), 169-85.

[279] Paul Boyer and Stephen Nissenbaum, *Salem-Village Witchcraft: A Documentary Record of Local Conflict in Colonial New England* (Boston: Northeastern University Press, 1993), 5.

[280] Richard B. Trask, *The Devil Hath Been Raised: A Documentary History of the Salem Village Witchcraft Outbreak of March 1692* (West Kennebunk, Maine: Phoenix Publishing, 1992), 4.

[281] Hansen, 37.

[282] Hansen, 37-8.

[283] Hansen, 38.

[284] Boyer and Nissenbaum, *Salem-Village Witchcraft*, 97.

[285] Trask, 30.

[286] Trask, 30.

[287] Boyer and Nissenbaum, *Salem Possessed*, 146.

[288] Trask, 38.

[289] Boyer and Nissenbaum, *Salem Possessed*, 182.f.

[290] Trask, 54.

[291] Trask, 58.

[292] Richard Godbeer, *The Devil's Dominion: Magic and Religion in Early New England* (Cambridge: Cambridge University Press, 1992), 203; Trask, ix.

[293] Rosenthal, 51; Hoffer, *The Devil's Disciples,* 100.

[294] Trask, 61.

[295] Reverend Deodat Lawson, *A Brief and True Narrative* (Boston: Benjamin Harris, 1692) in *Narratives of the Witchcraft Cases: 1648-1706,* ed. George Lincoln Burr (New York: Barnes & Noble, Inc., 1914, 1970), 162.

[296] Brian F. Le Beau, *The Story of the Salem Witch Trials: "We Walked in Clouds and Could Not See Our Way"* (Upper Saddle River, N.J.: Prentice Hall, 1998), 212.

[297] Michael G. Hall, *The Last American Puritan: The Life of Increase Mather, 1639-1723* (Middletown, CT: Wesleyan University Press, 1988), 249-52.

[298] Hall, *The Last American Puritan*, 253.

[299] Emerson W. Baker and John G. Reid, *The New England Knight: Sir William Phips, 1651-1695* (Toronto: University of Toronto Press, 1998), xi-xii.

[300] Baker and Reid, 144.

[301] David Levin, *What Happened in Salem: Documents Pertaining to the 17th Century Witchcraft Trials*, (New York: Twayne Publishers, 1950), 134.

[302] Enders A. Robinson, *The Devil Discovered: Salem Witchcraft 1692* (New York: Hippocrene Books, 1991), 229.

[303] Levin, 155-6.

[304] Baker and Reid, 145.

[305] Levin, 160-1.

[306] David Harley, "Explaining Salem: Calvinist Psychology and the Diagnosis of Possession," *American Historical Review* 101 (April 1996): 318.

[307] For more information on the loss of property and the accusations against powerful members of the Salem community, see David C. Brown, "The Forfeitures at Salem, 1692," *William and Mary Quarterly* 50 (1993): 85-111 and Bryan F. LeBeau, "Philip English and the Witchcraft Hysteria," *Historical Journal of Massachusetts* 15 (1987): 1-20.

[308] On the clergy's role in denouncing the trials, especially that of Reverend Samuel Willard, see David C. Brown, "The Salem Witchcraft Trials: Samuel Willard's *Some Miscellany Observations*," *Essex Institute Historical Collections* 122 (1986): 207-236 and Mark A. Peterson, "'Ordinary' Preaching and the Interpretation of the Salem Witchcraft Crisis by the Boston Clergy," *Essex Institute Historical Collections* 129 (1993): 84-102.

[309] Le Beau, 169.

[310] Robert Calef, *More Wonders of the Invisible World* (London: Nath. Hillar, 1700) in Burr, 358.

[311] Robinson, 35-6, 233-4.

[312] Robinson, 336-339.

[313] Hoffer, *The Devil Disciples*, 128-9.

[314] Harley, 320. For more information on the Mathers' participation in the witch trials, see David Levin, *Did the Mathers Disagree about the Salem Witchcraft Trials?* (Worcester, MA: American Antiquarian Society, 1985) and Richard H. Werking, "'Reformation Is Our Only Preservation': Cotton Mather and Salem Witchcraft," *William and Mary Quarterly* 29 (April 1972): 281-90.

[315] Le Beau, 209; Robinson, 240-2.

[316] For an interesting look at the importance of evidence other than spectral, see Wendel D. Craker, "Spectral Evidence, Non-Spectral Acts of Witchcraft, and Confession at Salem in 1692," *Historical Journal* 40 (1997): 331-358.

[317] Levin, 136.

[318] Rosenthal, 2,4.

[319] On the importance of folk beliefs and magic in colonial New England, see Richard Godbeer, *The Devil's Dominion: Magic and Religion in Early New England* (Cambridge: Cambridge University Press, 1992) and Richard Weisman, *Witchcraft, Magic and Religion in 17th Century Massachusetts* (Amherst, MA: The University of Massachusetts Press, 1984).

[320] Hall, *The Last American Puritan*, 251.

[321] David D. Hall, *Worlds of Wonder, Days of Judgment: Popular Religious Belief in Early New England* (New York: Alfred A. Knopf, 1989), 83-90; Increase Mather, *Remarkable Providences: An Essay for the Recording of Illustrious Providences* (Boston: 1684) in Burr, 8-13.

[322] Robert Middlekauff, *The Mathers: Three Generations of Puritan Intellectuals, 1596-1728* (New York: Oxford University Press, 1971), 148.

[323] On the tension these attacks caused, see James E. Kences, "Some Unexplored Relationships of Essex County Witchcraft to the Indian Wars of 1675 and 1689," *Essex Institute Historical Collections* 120 (1984): 179-212. For an intriguing and comprehensive interpretation of how the Indian attacks helped create the atmosphere that produced the events at Salem, see Mary Beth Norton, *In the Devil's Snare: The Salem Witchcraft Crisis of 1692* (New York: Alfred A. Knopf, 2002).

[324] Baker and Reid, 139.

[325] Baker and Reid, 141.

[326] Boyer and Nissenbaum, *Salem Possessed*, 86-88.

[327] Pauline Bartel, *Spellcasters: Witches & Witchcraft in History, Folklore & Popular Culture* (Dallas, Texas: Taylor Trade Publishing, 2000), 129; Boyer and Nissenbaum, *Salem Possessed*, 97-98.

[328] Hoffer, *The Devil's Disciples*, 42-6.

[329] Trask, xii.

[330] Bartel, 132.

[331] Larry Gragg, *A Quest For Security: The Life of Samuel Parris, 1653-1720* (New York: Greenwood Press, 1990), xvii-xviii, 93-99, 134-6; Frances Hill, *The Salem Witch Trials Reader* (Cambridge, MA: De Capo Press, 2000), 117-8; Hoffer, *The Devil's Disciples*, 61.

[332] Gragg, 134; Hoffer, *The Devil's Disciples*, 124.

[333] Reverend Samuel Parris, *The Sermon Notebook of Samuel Parris, 1689-1694,* eds. James F. Cooper and Kenneth P. Minkema (Boston: The Colonial Society of Massachusetts, 1993), 194-8.

[334] Hill, xv.

Conclusion: Common Patterns And Unanswered Questions

[335] Norman Gevitz, "'The Devil Hath Laughed at the Physicians': Witchcraft and Medical Practices in Seventeenth-Century New England," *Journal of the History of Medicine and Allied Sciences* 55 (January 2000): 18.

[336] Boyer and Nissenbaum, *Salem Possessed: The Social Origins of Witchcraft* (Cambridge, MA: Harvard University Press, 1974), 9.

[337] Gevitz, 18.

[338] *The Most Strange and Admirable Discoverie of the Three Witches of Warboys* (London: Widdowe Orwin, 1593), in *Witchcraft in England, 1558-1618*, ed. Barbara Rosen (Amherst, MA: The University of Massachusetts Press, 1969, 1991), 241.

[339] Stephen Bradwell, *Mary Glovers Late Woeful Case* (n. p., 1603) in Michael MacDonald, *Witchcraft and Hysteria in Elizabethan London: Edward Jorden and the Mary Glover Case* (London: Tavistock/Routledge, 1991), 17-9.

[340] D.P. Walker, *Unclean Spirits: Possession and Exorcism in France and England in the Late Sixteenth and Early Seventeenth Centuries* (Philadelphia: University of Pennsylvania Press, 1981), 62.

[341] *Most Strange and Admirable Discoverie*, in Rosen, 241.

[342] MacDonald, x.

[343] James Sharpe, *The Bewitching of Anne Gunter: A Horrible and True Story of Deception, Witchcraft, Murder and the King of England* (New York: Routledge, 2000), 6.

[344] For example, see Pauline Bartel, *Spellcasters: Witches & Witchcraft in History, Folklore & Popular Culture* (Dallas, Texas: Taylor Trade Publishing, 2000), 79-80; Chadwick Hansen, *Witchcraft at Salem* (New York: George Braziller, 1969), 31. Tituba's occult practices are also recounted on educational websites, such as National Geographic's interactive website on Salem: National Geographic Society, "Salem: Witchcraft Hysteria," 1997, **http://www.nationalgeographic.com/features/97/salem/** and the Discovery Channel's "Discovery School" website on Salem: Discovery.com, "Salem WitchTrials: The World

Behind the Hysteria, 2002, **http://school.discovery. com/schooladventures/salemwitchtrials/people/tituba.html**

[345] Bernard Rosenthal, *Salem Story: Reading the Witch Trials of 1692* (Cambridge: Cambridge University Press, 1993), 14.

[346] See the works cited in footnote 235, as well as Boyer and Nissenbaum, 1-2; Richard Godbeer, *The Devil's Dominion: Magic and Religion in Early New England* (Cambridge: Cambridge University Press, 1992), 34-5.

[347] Reverend John Hale, *A Modest Enquiry into the Nature of Witchcraft* (Boston: B. Eliot, 1702. Reprint, Bainbridge, N.Y.: York Mail-Print, 1973), 132-3. See also Hansen, 31.

[348] David D. Hall, *Worlds of Wonder, Days of Judgment: Popular Religious Belief in Early New England* (New York: Alfred A. Knopf, 1989), 99-100.

[349] Anne Reiber DeWindt "Witchcraft and Conflicting Visions of the Ideal Village Community," *Journal of British Studies* 34 (October 1995): 430-461. She argues on page 435 that the Throckmortons were "…purchasers of crown properties after the dissolution of the monasteries" and, as such, "…made a tragically unsuccessful attempt to "fit" into the social landscape of their fenland village."

[350] Gilbert Geis and Ivan Bunn, *A Trial of Witches: A Seventeenth-Century Witchcraft Prosecution* (London: Routledge, 1997), 13-20.

[351] Cotton Mather, *Memorable Providences, Relating to Witchcraft and Possessions* (Boston: R.P., 1689), in George Lincoln Burr, *Narratives of the Witchcraft Cases: 1648-1706* (New York: Barnes and Noble, Inc., 1914, 1970), 99.

[352] Mather in Burr, 101.

[353] Sharpe, 90-101.

[354] Alan Macfarlane, *Witchcraft in Tudor and Stuart England: A Regional and Comparative Study* (Prospect Heights, Illinois: Waveland Press, 1970), 158-176.

[355] Macfarlane, 158-9.

[356] MacDonald, 48.

[357] Boyer and Nissenbaum, 205.

[358] Moira Tatem, *The Witches of Warboys* (Cambridgeshire, U.K.: Cambridgeshire Libraries Publications, 1993), 19.

[359] Mather in Burr, 100, 103.

[360] Hansen, 64; Sharpe, xi.

[361] Macfarlane, 168-9.

[362] Macfarlane, 162-3.

[363] Macfarlane, 164.

[364] Macfarlane, 164.

[365] Tatem, 18.

[366] John Swan, *A True and Briefe Report of Mary Glovers Vexation* (n.p., 1603) in MacDonald, 46-7.

[367] Mather in Burr, 100, 102.

[368] Mather in Burr, 110.

[369] Steven Bradwell, *Mary Glovers Late Woeful Case* (n.p., 1603) in MacDonald, 114.

[370] Sharpe, 103.

[371] Frances Hill, *The Salem Witch Trials Reader* (Cambridge, MA: De Capo Press, 2000), 108.

Bibliography

Baker, Emerson W., and John G. Reid. *The New England Knight: Sir William Phips, 1651-1695.* Toronto: University of Toronto Press, 1998.

Bartel, Pauline. *Spellcasters: Witches & Witchcraft in History, Folklore & Popular Culture.* Dallas, Texas: Taylor Trade Publishing, 2000.

Bostridge, Ian. *Witchcraft and Its Transformations: 1650-1750.* Oxford: Clarendon Press, 1997.

Boyer, Paul, and Stephen Nissenbaum. *Salem Possessed: The Social Origins of Witchcraft.* Cambridge, MA: Harvard University Press, 1974.

Boyer, Paul, and Stephen Nissenbaum. *Salem-Village Witchcraft: A Documentary Record of Local Conflict in Colonial New England.* Boston: Northeastern University Press, 1993.

Breslaw, Elaine G. *Witches of the Atlantic World: A Historical Reader & Primary Sourcebook.* New York: New York University Press, 2000.

Briggs, Robin. *Witches & Neighbors: The Social and Cultural Context of European Witchcraft.* New York: Viking, 1996.

Browne, Sir Thomas. *This Special Edition of Religio Medici.* Birmingham, AL: The Classics of Medicine Library, 1981.

Brownlow, F.W. *Shakespeare, Harsnett, and the Devils of Denham.* Newark: University of Delaware Press, 1993.

Burr, George Lincoln. *Narratives of the Witchcraft Cases, 1648-1706.* New York: C. Scribner's Sons, 1914.

Caciola, Nancy. "Mystics, Demoniacs, and the Physiology of Spirit Possession in Medieval Europe." *Comparative Studies in Society and History* 42 (April 2000): 268-306.

Camden, Carroll. "The Suffocation of the Mother." *Modern Language Notes* 63 (June 1948): 390-3.

Caporael, Linnda R. "Ergotism: The Satan Loosed in Salem." *Science* 192 (April 2, 1976): 21-6.

Carlson, Laurie Winn. *A Fever in Salem: A New Interpretation of the New England Witch Trials.* Chicago: Ivan R. Dee, 1999.

Clark, Stuart. *Thinking With Demons: The Idea of Witchcraft in Early Modern Europe.* Oxford: Oxford University Press, 1997.

Cromartie, Alan. *Sir Mathew Hale: 1609-1676.* Cambridge: Cambridge University Press, 1995.

Davies, Stevan L. *Jesus the Healer: Possession, Trance, and the Origins of Christianity.* New York: The Continuum Publishing Company, 1995.

Demos, John Putnam. *Entertaining Satan.* Oxford: Oxford University Press, 1982.

DeWindt, Anne Reiber. "Witchcraft and Conflicting Visions of the Ideal Village Community." *Journal of British Studies* 34 (October 1995): 427-61.

Drake, Frederick C. "Witchcraft in the American Colonies, 1647-62," *American Quarterly* 20 (Winter, 1968): 701-715.

Dunn, William Parmly. *Sir Thomas Browne: A Study in Religious Philosophy.* MN: University of Minnesota Press, 1950.

Erikson, Kai T. *Wayward Puritans: A Study in the Sociology of Deviance.* New York: John Wiley & Sons, 1966.

Fox, Sanford J. *Science and Justice: The Massachusetts Witchcraft Trials.* Baltimore: Johns Hopkins Press, 1968.

Geis, Gilbert. "Sir Thomas Browne and Witchcraft: A Cautionary Tale for Contemporary Law and Psychiatry" *International Journal of Law and Psychiatry* (4 1981): 1-11.

Geis, Gilbert and Bunn, Ivan. *A Trial of Witches: A Seventeenth-Century Witchcraft Prosecution.* London: Routledge, 1997.

Gibson, Marion. *Reading Witchcraft: Stories of Early English Witches.* London: Routledge, 1999.

Godbeer, Richard. *The Devil's Dominion: Magic and Religion in Early New England.* Cambridge: Cambridge University Press, 1992.

Gosse, Edmund. *Sir Thomas Browne.* London: Macmillan and Co., Limited, 1924.

Gragg, Larry. *A Quest for Security: The Life of Samuel Parris, 1653-1720.* New York: Greenwood Press, 1990.

Greenblatt, Stephen. "Exorcism Into Art." *Representations* 12 (Autumn 1985): 15-23.

Guiley, Rosemary Ellen. *The Encyclopedia of Witches and Witchcraft.* 2nd edition. New York: Checkmark Books, 1999.

Hale, John. *A Modest Enquiry Into The Nature Of Witchcraft.* Boston: B. Eliot, 1702. Reprint, Bainbridge, N.Y.: York Mail-Print, 1973.

Hall, David D. *Witch-Hunting in Seventeenth-Century New England.* Boston: Northeastern University Press, 1991.

Hall, David D. *Worlds of Wonder, Days of Judgment: Popular Religious Belief in Early New England.* New York: Alfred A. Knopf, 1989.

Hall, Michael G. *The Last American Puritan: The Life of Increase Mather, 1639-1723.* Middletown, CT: Wesleyan University Press, 1988.

Hansen, Chadwick. *Witchcraft at Salem.* New York: George Braziller, 1969.

Harley, David. "Explaining Salem: Calvinist Psychology and the Diagnosis of Possession." *The American Historical Review* 101 (April 1996): 307-330.

Heward, Edmund. *Matthew Hale.* London: Robert Hale & Company, 1972.

Hill, Frances. *A Delusion of Satan: The Full Story of the Salem Witch Trials.* New York: Doubleday, 1995.

Hill, Frances. *The Salem Witch Trials Reader.* Cambridge, MA: De Capo Press, 2000.

Hoffer, Peter Charles. *The Devil's Disciples: Makers of the Salem Witchcraft Trials.* Baltimore: Johns Hopkins University Press, 1996.

Hoffer, Peter Charles. *The Salem Witchcraft Trials: A Legal History.* Lawrence, Kansas: University Press of Kansas, 1997.

Holmes, Ronald. *Witchcraft in British History.* London: Frederick Muller Limited, 1974.

Karlsen, Carol F. *The Devil in the Shape of a Woman: Witchcraft in Colonial New England.* New York: W.W. Norton & Company, 1998.

Kemp, Simon, and Kevin Williams. "Demonic Possession and Mental Disorders in Medieval and Early Modern Europe." *Psychological Medicine* 17 (1987): 21-9.

Kinney Arthur F. and David W. Swain, eds., *Tudor England: An Encyclopedia.* New York and London: Garland Publishing, 2001.

Kittredge, George Lyman. *Witchcraft in Old and New England.* Cambridge, MA: Harvard University Press, 1929.

Klaits, Joseph. *Servants of Satan: The Age of the Witch Hunts.* Bloomington, Ind.: Indiana University Press, 1985.

Larner, Christine. *Witchcraft and Religion: The Politics of Popular Belief.* New York: Basil Blackwell, 1984.

Le Beau, Brian F. *The Story of the Salem Witch Trials: "We Walked In Clouds and Could Not See Our Way."* Upper Saddle River, N.J.: Prentice Hall, 1998.

Levack, Brian P. ed., *Possession and Exorcism.* New York: Garland Publishing, 1992.

Levack, Brian P. "Possession, Witchcraft, and the Law in Jacobean England." *Washington and Lee Law Review* 52 (1996): 1613-40.

Levack, Brian P., ed. *Witchcraft in Colonial America.* New York: Garland Publishing, 1992.

Levack, Brian P., ed. *The Witch-hunt in Early Modern Europe.* New York: Garland Publishing, 1987.

Levin, David. *Cotton Mather: The Young Life of the Lord's Remembrancer, 1663-1703*. Cambridge, MA: Harvard University Press, 1978.

Levin, David. *Did the Mathers Disagree about the Salem Witchcraft Trials?* Worcester, MA: American Antiquarian Society, 1985.

Levin, David, ed. *What Happened At Salem: Documents Pertaining to the 17th Century Witchcraft Trials*. New York: Twayne Publishers, 1952.

MacDonald, Michael. *Witchcraft and Hysteria in Elizabethan London: Edward Jorden and the Mary Glover case*. London: Tavistock/Routledge, 1991.

Macfarlane, Alan. *Witchcraft in Tudor and Stuart England: A Regional and Comparative Study*. Prospect Heights, Illinois: Waveland Press, 1970.

Mappen, Marc, ed. *Witches and Historians*. Malabar, Fla.: Krieger Publisher, 1996.

Marshman, Michelle. "Exorcism as Empowerment: A New Idiom." *The Journal of Religious History* 23 (October 1999): 265-281.

Marwick, Max, ed. *Witchcraft and Sorcery*. London: Penguin Books, 1982.

Mather, Cotton. *Wonders of the Invisible World*. London: John Russell Smith, 1862.

Middlekauff, Robert. *The Mathers: Three Generations of Puritan Intellectuals, 1596-1728*. New York: Oxford University Press, 1971.

Monter, E. William. *Ritual, Myth and Magic in Early Modern Europe*. Athens, Ohio: Ohio University Press, 1984.

"The Most Strange and Admirable Discoverie of the Three Witches of Warboys." London: Widdowe Orwin, 1593. In *Witchcraft in England, 1558-1618*. Edited by Barbara Rosen, 239-297. Amherst, MA: University of Massachusetts Press, 1991.

Parris, Reverend Samuel. *The Sermon Notebook of Samuel Parris, 1689-1694*. Edited by James F. Cooper and Kenneth P. Minkema. Boston: The Colonial Society of Massachusetts, 1993.

Pearl, Jonathan L. "'A School for the Rebel Soul': Politics and Demonic Possession in France." *Historical Reflections* 16 (1989): 286-306.

Peterson, Mark A. "'Ordinary' Preaching and the Interpretation of the Salem Witchcraft Crisis by the Boston Clergy." *Essex Institute Historical Collection* 129 (1993): 84-102.

Raiswell, Richard. "'Faking It': A Case of Counterfeit Possession in the Reign of James I." *Renaissance and Reformation* 23 (Summer 1999): 29-48.

Reis, Elizabeth. *Damned Women: Sinners and Witches in Puritan New England*. Ithaca, N.Y.: Cornell University Press, 1997.

Reis, Elizabeth, ed. *Spellbound: Women and Witchcraft in America*. Wilmington, Delaware: SR Books, 1998.

Rickert, Corinne Holt. *The Case of John Darrell: Minister and Exorcist*. Gainesville: University of Florida Press, 1962.

Robbins, Rossell Hope. *The Encyclopedia of Witchcraft and Demonology*. New York: Crown Publishers, 1959.

Robinson, Enders A. *The Devil Discovered: Salem Witchcraft 1692*. New York: Hippocrene Books, 1991.

Rosenthal, Bernard. *Salem Story: Reading the Witch Trials of 1692.* Cambridge: Cambridge University Press, 1993.

Sharpe, James. *The Bewitching of Anne Gunter: A Horrible and True Story of Deception, Witchcraft, Murder and the King of England.* New York: Routledge, 2000.

Sharpe, James. *Instruments of Darkness: Witchcraft in Early Modern England.* Philadelphia: University of Pennsylvania Press, 1996.

Silverman, Kenneth. *The Life and Times of Cotton Mather.* New York: Harper & Row, 1984.

Sluhovsky, Moshe. "A Divine Apparition or Demonic Possession? Female Agency and Church Authority in Sixteenth-Century France." *Sixteenth Century Journal* 27 (1996): 1039-1055.

Spanos, Nicholas P. *Multiple Identities and False Memories.* Washington, D.C.: American Psychological Association, 1996.

Stephen, Sir Leslie and Sir Sidney Lee, eds., *The Dictionary of National Biography.* London: Oxford University Press, 1917.

Tatem, Moira. *Witches of Warboys.* Cambridgeshire, U.K.: Cambridgeshire Libraries Publications, 1993.

Thomas, Keith. *Religion and the Decline of Magic.* New York: Charles Scribner's Sons, 1971.

Tourney, G. "The Physician and witchcraft in restoration England" *Medical History* 16 (April 1972): 143-155.

Trask, Richard B. *"The Devil Hath Been Raised": A Documentary History of the Salem Village Outbreak of March 1692.* West Kennebunk, Maine: Phoenix Publishing, 1992.

Veith, Ilza. *Hysteria: The History of a Disease*. Chicago: University of Chicago Press, 1965.

Walker, D.P. *Unclean Spirits: Possession and Exorcism in France and England in the Late Sixteenth and Early Seventeenth Centuries*. Philadelphia: University of Pennsylvania Press, 1981.

Watson, Patricia A. *The Angelical Conjunction: The Preacher-Physicians of Colonial New England*. Knoxville, Tenn.: The University of Tennessee Press, 1991.

Willis, Deborah. *Malevolent Nurture: Witch-Hunting and Maternal Power in Early Modern England*. Ithaca: Cornell University Press, 1995.

Woolf, Alan. "Witchcraft or Mycotoxin? The Salem Witch Trials," *Journal of Toxicology. Clinical Toxicology* 38 (2000): 457-60.

0-595-26589-8

Printed in Great Britain
by Amazon